Number 117
Spring 2008

New Directions for Evaluation

Sandra Mathison
Editor-in-Chief

Consequences of No Child Left Behind for Educational Evaluation

Tiffany Berry
Rebecca M. Eddy
Editors

1920120014

CONSEQUENCES OF NO CHILD LEFT BEHIND FOR EDUCATIONAL
EVALUATION
Tiffany Berry, Rebecca M. Eddy (eds.)
New Directions for Evaluation, no. 117
Sandra Mathison, Editor-in-Chief

Microfilm copies of issues and articles are available in 16mm and 35mm,
as well as microfiche in 105mm, through University Microfilms Inc., 300
North Zeeb Road, Ann Arbor, Michigan 48106-1346.

New Directions for Evaluation is indexed in Cambridge Scientific Abstracts
(CSA/CIG), Contents Pages in Education (T & F), Educational Research
Abstracts Online (T & F), ERIC Database (Education Resources
Information Center), Higher Education Abstracts (Claremont Graduate
University), Social Services Abstracts (CSA/CIG), Sociological Abstracts
(CSA/CIG), and Worldwide Political Sciences Abstracts (CSA/CIG).

NEW DIRECTIONS FOR EVALUATION (ISSN 1097-6736, electronic ISSN
1534-875X) is part of The Jossey-Bass Education Series and is published
quarterly by Wiley Subscription Services, Inc., A Wiley Company, at
Jossey-Bass, 989 Market Street, San Francisco, California 94103-1741.

SUBSCRIPTIONS cost $85 for U.S./Canada/Mexico; $109 international.
For institutions, agencies, and libraries, $215 U.S.; $255 Canada/Mexico;
$289 international. Prices subject to change.

EDITORIAL CORRESPONDENCE should be addressed to the Editor-in-Chief,
Sandra Mathison, University of British Columbia, 2125 Main Mall,
Vancouver, BC V6T 1Z4, Canada.

www.josseybass.com

Editorial Policy and Procedures

New Directions for Evaluation, a quarterly sourcebook, is an official publication of the American Evaluation Association. The journal publishes empirical, methodological, and theoretical works on all aspects of evaluation. A reflective approach to evaluation is an essential strand to be woven through every volume. The editors encourage volumes that have one of three foci: (1) craft volumes that present approaches, methods, or techniques that can be applied in evaluation practice, such as the use of templates, case studies, or survey research; (2) professional issue volumes that present issues of import for the field of evaluation, such as utilization of evaluation or locus of evaluation capacity; (3) societal issue volumes that draw out the implications of intellectual, social, or cultural developments for the field of evaluation, such as the women's movement, communitarianism, or multiculturalism. A wide range of substantive domains is appropriate for *New Directions for Evaluation;* however, the domains must be of interest to a large audience within the field of evaluation. We encourage a diversity of perspectives and experiences within each volume, as well as creative bridges between evaluation and other sectors of our collective lives.

The editors do not consider or publish unsolicited single manuscripts. Each issue of the journal is devoted to a single topic, with contributions solicited, organized, reviewed, and edited by a guest editor. Issues may take any of several forms, such as a series of related chapters, a debate, or a long article followed by brief critical commentaries. In all cases, the proposals must follow a specific format, which can be obtained from the editor-in-chief. These proposals are sent to members of the editorial board and to relevant substantive experts for peer review. The process may result in acceptance, a recommendation to revise and resubmit, or rejection. However, the editors are committed to working constructively with potential guest editors to help them develop acceptable proposals.

Sandra Mathison, Editor-in-Chief
University of British Columbia
2125 Main Mall
Vancouver, BC V6T 1Z4
CANADA
e-mail: nde@eval.org

CONTENTS

EDITORS' NOTES

Under No Child Left Behind (NCLB, 2001), as well as other federal accountability systems, evaluation is often used as a tool to help achieve legislative goals. Core aspects of the legislation (for example, measuring school and district academic progress, setting performance standards, using data to inform instruction, monitoring learning outcomes, and so on) are a few of the ways in which evaluative activities have become integrated into the fabric of NCLB's educational accountability system. One plausible consequence of this close integration is that the purpose, design, and practice of evaluation may actually become *transformed* by accountability systems, especially if the context in which evaluation is implemented is specific, mandated by law, or required. This issue of *New Directions for Evaluation* describes these transformative influences and explores their potential consequences. Within the chapters, we hear perspectives from evaluation practitioners who have extensive experience working within schools, districts, and community-based programs, as well as from a textbook publisher, educational assessment specialists, and university professors. These multiple perspectives allow us to explore the various pathways by which NCLB legislation affects the field of evaluation.

No Child Left Behind and Educational Evaluation

President George W. Bush signed NCLB into law on January 8, 2002, as a reauthorization of the Elementary and Secondary Education Act (ESEA). Although a comprehensive review of the legislation is provided in chapter 1 of this volume, briefly NCLB consists of four primary pillars: (1) stronger accountability for results through the use of standards, academic achievement assessments, and sanctions for schools and districts that do not meet academic performance standards; (2) more freedom for states and

---

Note: We would like to acknowledge colleagues and friends who were instrumental in helping us complete this volume. Sandra Mathison, our editor-in-chief, helped develop the ideas that came to fruition in the volume and offered her continuing encouragement and patience. Tina Christie and Mel Mark joined initial discussions of our ideas, and anonymous reviewers gave insightful guidance in moving the ideas forward. We especially appreciate working with the chapter authors who contributed to this volume. Finally, we would also like to thank our families, in particular Eric, Dylan, and Brooke Berry and Richard Eddy, for their continued patience, love, and support through this process and in all of our work.

communities, driven primarily through flexibility in the use of federal funds; (3) proven education methods, especially in conducting rigorous, experimental research on educational programs and materials; and (4) more choices for parents to access supplemental education services for low-performing students and/or to move their students to higher performing schools within the district.

Given the controversial nature of NCLB and its core tenets, an extensive body of literature has accumulated over the past few years. A steady stream of commentaries, critiques, and debates about whether the legislation is working, who it is working for, how should it be implemented, how student performance should be measured, and so on, has dominated educational circles (Hall & Kennedy, 2006; Hoff & Manzo, 2007; Lee, 2006; Reid, 2005). In addition, the educational research and evaluation literature has examined the consequences of the legislation on such issues as democratic evaluation (Ryan, 2002), the role of high-stakes testing (Amrein & Berliner, 2002), student academic achievement (Northwest Evaluation Association, 2005), and the influence of rigorous, scientific methods in educational research (Eisenhart & Towne, 2003). However, this expanded body of literature fails to examine how evaluation practitioners navigate through legislative requirements, mandates, sanctions, and the like. As a result, it is unclear how their evaluation practice potentially influences the purpose, design, and practice of educational evaluation. This is important, given that it is less common to discuss examples of how the *context* in which evaluators practice influences the discipline of evaluation; rather, more often we see examples from the evaluation community recommending how evaluations should be conducted (see Huffman & Lawrenz, 2006), how to implement an evaluation theorist's perspective in practice (Alkin & Christie, 2005), or even what issues should be incorporated into evaluation practice, such as promoting inclusion (Mertens, 1999), increasing use in organizations (Torres & Preskill, 2001), or upholding democratic principles (House & Howe, 2000). Although these intellectual pursuits are necessary to propel the field forward, this volume is an opportunity to explore how key aspects of the legislation have transformed the landscape of educational evaluation, and ultimately how this process is redefining what evaluation is within the educational evaluation community.

Transformative Influences and Evaluative Consequences

Two pillars of NCLB, in particular, have transformed the landscape of educational evaluation: stronger accountability for results and proven education methods. In fact, these two pillars are the driving, transformative influences that, we believe, most affect educational evaluation. The first, stronger accountability for results, lies in states' implementing an assessment system that includes three primary components: (1) developing challenging academic content standards across disciplines; (2) implementing annual assessments that track student proficiency levels in reading, mathematics, and science; and (3) imposing sanctions on schools and districts for not meeting academic performance goals. The second transformative influence concerns "proven education methods." Specifically, this involves implementing scientifically based research (SBR); according to the U.S. Department of Education (2003), . . ."using an experimental design [is] best for determining project effectiveness. . . . Proposed evaluation strategies that use neither experimental designs with random assignment nor quasi-experimental designs using a matched comparison group nor regression discontinuity designs will not be considered responsive to the [federal] priority when sufficient numbers of participants are available to support these designs" (p. 62446).

Together, these two key components of NCLB have influenced how evaluation is conducted in schools, districts, publishing houses, and community-based programs. Using NCLB as a backdrop, evaluation practitioners with extensive experience in the field explore the consequences of these transformative influences through case studies, critical commentaries, and technical information related to the nexus between evaluation and NCLB (that is, measuring student achievement under NCLB). Although it is not our intention to establish a causal relationship between NCLB and changes in evaluation practice, this volume does represent reasonable claims that we, as well as several of our contributing authors, have witnessed in conducting evaluations while navigating the legislative requirements of NCLB. This volume explores several essential questions relevant to educational evaluators:

- How do educational evaluators operate effectively within NCLB?
- What techniques, tools, and methods are commonly used in responding to NCLB requirements?
- What are the common challenges facing evaluation professionals working in schools, districts, and other educational programs?
- Which specific parts of the legislation have the greatest impact on evaluators, and what are some of the consequences?
- What are the opportunity costs associated with conducting research and evaluation as prescribed under NCLB?
- What are the opportunities afforded to the evaluation community as a result of the nexus between NCLB and evaluation practice?

Additionally, although this volume is specifically geared toward NCLB, the broader concept of accountability and evidenced-based practice has infiltrated several disciplines, notably nursing, management, and nonprofit sectors (see Donaldson, Christie, & Mark, in press). Consequently, we hope that this volume stimulates conversation around fundamental issues in the discipline of evaluation, such as blurring the lines among research, evaluation, and assessment; prioritizing summative over formative evaluations; using questions to drive research designs rather than the reverse; balancing accountability requirements with other stakeholder needs; exploring the role of evaluation capacity building within institutional settings; availability and appropriate use of assessment data; and defining learning outcomes that are based on standardized test scores alone.

Caveats, Clarifications, and Assumptions

Given the highly politicized nature of NCLB, it is important to place this volume within the context in which it was intended. First, given our professional practice, educational backgrounds, and academic appointments, we believe the impact of NCLB on educational evaluation is neither entirely positive nor entirely negative, but rather is complex. We welcome more discussion surrounding the appropriateness of specific evaluation designs and educational research infused with increased scientific rigor. However, we are concerned (as are others in the evaluation community; see Julnes & Rog, 2007) that the choice of method dictates the evaluation design rather than the evaluation questions. In addition, insistence on experimental designs in some settings is also problematic because it may devalue other types of appropriate, yet nonexperimental, designs. Finally, we are increasingly concerned that the current structure of educational accountability systems may relegate the philosophical purpose of evaluation to an audit function, and as a result, in our view, may undermine the primary purpose of evaluation: determining the merit, worth, or significance of the evaluand (Scriven, 1991).

To address this complexity, we have assembled a group of contributing authors who are experienced in the field of educational evaluation and who understand the critical issues facing the field in light of NCLB. Surprisingly, recruiting contributing authors proved to be more difficult than we initially anticipated, given that many evaluators, organizations, and county offices of education were hesitant to contribute to this volume for fear of political backlash in stating their views publicly. Despite this, this volume includes a strong group of authors who could constructively contribute to this academic discussion by being fair, balanced, critical, and reflective.

Second, although this volume is focused specifically on NCLB, it is clear that NCLB is the result of a movement over the last several decades toward increasing educational accountability and performance standards. Indeed, to place NCLB in its proper context, the first chapter of the volume traces the evolution of NCLB through prior legislation as well as discusses the precursors to accountability (that is, assessment and standards). This suggests that the consequences described in this volume may or may not specifically stem from NCLB, but rather come from the broader movement in educational accountability established decades ago.

NEW DIRECTIONS FOR EVALUATION • DOI: 10.1002/ev

Third, given the breadth of this volume, several relevant issues were intentionally omitted. For example, the debate about whether standardized test scores yield a fair assessment of student learning is not specifically addressed in this volume, although ensuring that the measures evaluators use to document learning outcomes accurately reflect the constructs is certainly not a trivial point for educators or evaluators. However, within this volume we have addressed the need to rely on multiple measures of student learning to appropriately gauge student outcomes. Another issue that has been omitted is discussion of the feasibility of schools meeting Adequate Yearly Progress (AYP) requirements within the timeline specified by NCLB, or ever. No one can accurately predict the extent to which schools will be able to meet Annual Measurable Objectives (AMOs) in the coming years. Similarly, we have omitted whether NCLB has successfully improved student achievement and met the intended outcomes of the legislation. Although these issues were beyond the scope of the current volume, they could have just as easily occupied some of these pages.

Fourth, it is important to note that the experiences of the evaluation practitioners herein may not be generalizable or representative, but idiosyncratic. We have included case studies in an effort to describe issues practitioners are facing daily related to NCLB, with the specific intention of identifying cross-cutting themes that generalize past the local context (an issue we explore in depth in Chapter Eight of this volume). Similarly, it is important to note that the flavor of the volume might have differed if other potential perspectives had been included (Government Accounting Office, the Institute of Educational Sciences, Office of Management and Budget).

Organization of the Volume

The volume is organized into three sections in addition to a concluding chapter. The first section (chapters 1 and 2) has overview chapters, designed to orient the reader to the larger issues related to NCLB and evaluation. In chapter 1, Jack Mills, an evaluator and governing board member for Claremont Unified School District in California, describes the key issues in the legislation as well as reviews possible reauthorization changes that may occur in 2008. Linda Mabry, an experienced evaluator who has been active in challenging the federal priority for scientifically based research, discusses how NCLB has influenced the purpose, design, and impact of evaluation (chapter 2).

The second section (chapters 3, 4, and 5) includes specific case studies of how evaluators and the schools, districts, and educational programs they serve have addressed challenges related to both accountability systems and SBR. Chapter 3 describes how one local school instituted intense professional development in an effort to implement specific strategies around using data to improve instruction. This chapter was written by the school's former assistant principal, Meta Nelson (now at the district), and the school's evaluator, Rebecca M. Eddy. In chapter 4, Lisa N. T. Schmitt and Maria Defino Whitsett describe the challenges faced by local school district evaluators in Texas, a particularly interesting case given the dual (and sometimes competing) accountability systems in which they operate. To demonstrate how NCLB has even affected evaluation of community-based programs that are school-linked, chapter 5 describes how one after-school program's evaluation has adapted questions, designs, and methods in response to NCLB. This chapter was written by three practicing evaluators, Blanca Flor Guillén-Woods, Monica A. Kaiser, and Maura J. Harrington.

The third section has examples of other key areas of the legislation relevant to evaluators. Specifically, Mariam Azin and Miriam G. Resendez address challenges related to using assessment data in evaluations in chapter 6. Chapter 7 presents a perspective that is not often heard, that of textbook publishers, in which Marcy Baughman, the director of academic research at Pearson Education, describes current issues related to textbook adoption and research that must meet the federal priority as "scientifically based." The final chapter, written by Rebecca M. Eddy and Tiffany Berry, summarizes the challenges in educational evaluation and NCLB presented throughout the volume and extends them into opportunities for the discipline of evaluation.

Overall, this volume of *New Directions for Evaluation* reviews some of the most critical issues in the field of educational evaluation under NCLB. We look forward to extending the conversation regarding how the transforming influence of NCLB will continue to shape our practice as well as the practice of schools, districts, and programs that we serve.

References

Alkin, M., & Christie, C. (2005). *Theorists' models in action. New Directions for Evaluation, 106.*

Amrein, A. L., & Berliner, D. C. (2002). High-stakes testing, uncertainty, and student learning. *Education Policy Analysis Archives, 10*(18).

Donaldson, S. I., Christie, C. A., & Mark, M. M. (in press). *What counts as credible evidence in applied research and contemporary evaluation practice?* Newbury Park, CA: Sage.

Eisenhart, M., & Towne, L. (2003). Contestation and change in national policy on scientifically based education research. *Educational Researcher, 31*(7), 31–38.

Hall, D., & Kennedy, S. (2006). *Primary progress, secondary challenge: A state-by-state look at student achievement patterns.* Washington, DC: Education Trust.

Hoff, D. J., & Manzo, K. K. (2007). Bush claims about NCLB questioned: Data on gains in achievement remain limited, preliminary. *Education Week, 26*, 26–27.

House, E. R., & Howe, K. R. (2000). Deliberative, democratic evaluation. In K. E. Ryan & L. DeStefano (Eds.), *Evaluation as a democratic process: Promoting inclusion, dialogue, and deliberation. New Directions for Evaluation, 85*, 3–12

Huffman, D., & Lawrenz, F. (2006). *Critical issues in STEM evaluation. New Directions for Evaluation, 109.*

Julnes, G., & Rog, D. J. (2007). *Informing federal policies on evaluation methodology: Building the evidence base for method choice in government sponsored evaluation. New Directions for Evaluation, 113.*

Lee, J. (2006). *Tracking achievement gaps and assessing the impact of NCLB on the gaps: An in-depth look into national and state reading and math outcome trends.* Cambridge, MA: Civil Rights Project, Harvard University.

Mertens, D. M. (1999). Inclusive evaluation: Implications of transformative theory for evaluation. *American Journal of Evaluation, 20,* 1–14.

No Child Left Behind Act. (2001). Public Law No. 107–110. 107th Congress, 110 *Congressional Record* 1425, 115 Stat.

Northwest Evaluation Association. (2005). *The impact of the No Child Left Behind Act on student achievement and growth: 2005 edition.* Portland, OR: Northwest Evaluation Association.

Reid, K. S. (2005). Civil rights groups split over NCLB: Accountability provisions stirring heated debate. *Education Week, 25,* 20–21.

Ryan, K. (2002). Shaping educational accountability systems. *American Journal of Evaluation, 23,* 453–468.

Scriven, M. (1991). *Evaluation thesaurus* (4th ed). Thousand Oaks, CA: Sage.

Torres, R. T., & Preskill, H. (2001). Evaluation and organizational learning: Past, present, and future. *American Journal of Evaluation, 22,* 387–395.

U.S. Department of Education. (2003). Notice of proposed priority: Scientifically based evaluation methods (RIN 1890-ZA00). *Federal Register, 68*(213), 62445–62447.

Tiffany Berry
Rebecca M. Eddy
Editors

TIFFANY BERRY is a practicing educational evaluator and research assistant professor in the School of Behavioral and Organizational Sciences at Claremont Graduate University.

REBECCA M. EDDY is an evaluator of educational programs and research assistant professor in the School of Behavioral and Organizational Sciences at Claremont Graduate University.

Mills, J. I. (2008). A legislative overview of No Child Left Behind. In T. Berry & R. M. Eddy (Eds.), *Consequences of No Child Left Behind for educational evaluation. New Directions for Evaluation, 117*, 9–20.

1

A Legislative Overview of No Child Left Behind

Jack I. Mills

Abstract

No Child Left Behind (NCLB), the reauthorization of the Elementary and Secondary Education Act, was passed in 2002. This legislation broadly states federal policy regarding education and is situated within the historical context of Lyndon Johnson's Great Society programs. Like any federal legislation, NCLB consists of the legislation itself but also the procedures established by the U.S. Department of Education and interpretations of the legislation at the local education-authority level. The author describes two of the four pillars of the legislation most relevant for evaluators: accountability requirements and application of rigorous scientific research. With the impending reauthorization of NCLB, possible changes to the legislation are discussed. © Wiley Periodicals, Inc.

President George W. Bush signed No Child Left Behind (NCLB, 2001) into law on January 8, 2002. NCLB is a reauthorization of the Elementary and Secondary Education Act (ESEA) and is set for reauthorization in 2008. Given the anticipated reauthorization as well as a need for the research community to understand specifics contained within the legislation, this chapter explains the critical pieces of NCLB that are relevant to

evaluators. The primary focus is on elements of NCLB related to two of its four pillars, specifically, accountability requirements and application of rigorous scientific research. Although NCLB's objectives and methods have sparked controversy within public education circles, the public policy arena, and the evaluation field (Boruch, 2007; Chelimsky, 2007; Smith, 2005; West, 2005), this overview is intended to be an objective summary of the legislation.

Originally part of Lyndon Johnson's Great Society program, ESEA made available extra resources to help high-poverty schools provide the same educational opportunities as other non-high-poverty schools. ESEA expanded the role for the federal government in a public education system that remains largely funded and managed by individual states and their constituent school districts—also known as local educational authorities (LEAs). Technically, NCLB applies only to schools or districts that receive federal funding authorized through NCLB (typically Title I), but its provisions have certainly set a tone throughout educational research communities. Some LEAs may wish to forgo ESEA/NCLB funding in order to avoid some of the more onerous provisions of the law (such as the requirement that 100% of students reach proficiency by 2014), but the $2.8 billion that various ESEA/NCLB titles bring to California alone (EdSource, 2007) makes it hard for LEAs, especially those in low-income areas, to turn away their share of that support.

One must look to several sources to understand fully how NCLB is to be implemented. The primary source is the law itself, officially known as Public Law 107–110 (NCLB, 2001). Another layer of interpretation is added as the executive branch of the U.S. government, in this case, the Department of Education (DOE), develops regulations and operating guidelines to instruct states and LEAs as to exactly how the law should be implemented (Department of Education, 2002). Next, the DOE has negotiated a plan with each state for complying with NCLB, although the exact implementation of NCLB varies by state (Center on Education Policy, 2007). Finally, given both federal and state frameworks, there may be variations among LEAs and individual school sites regarding the practices put in place to respond to the law's requirements.

Some of the most notable features of the act are (1) accountability requirements by which schools must demonstrate Adequate Yearly Progress (AYP) based on students reaching targets for achievement (known as Annual Measurable Objectives, or AMOs) as measured by standardized tests and other indicators; (2) consequences for schools failing to meet AYP along with options for students in these schools to receive supplemental educational services (SES) and transportation to higher performing, or safer, schools within the same school district; (3) application of rigorous scientifically based research (SBR) standards to educational programs and practices to ensure that students are exposed to teaching strategies and methods for which a strong evidence base exists; and (4) requirements that teachers and paraprofessionals must meet "highly qualified" educational and credentialing criteria to remain in the classroom. This is a condensed list. The full bill includes funding and requirements for numerous other educational programs, among them Indian and Native Hawaiian and Alaskan education, language instruction for limited English proficiency children, and several other community-based educational programs (as an example, the William F. Goodling Even Start Program).

The Evolution of Accountability, Standards, and Assessment

The notion of accountability for outcomes is not unique to public education or to NCLB. Examples of the trend toward evidence-based practices are found in many fields (Donaldson, Christie, & Mark, in press), such as management and health care. In the social service sector, the W. K. Kellogg Foundation (1998) is known for its focus on rigorous evaluation research. Within public education, historical reviews (Mathison, 2005; McDonnell, 2005) show that the move toward the performance monitoring and accountability provisions reflected in NCLB has been a gradual evolution over time rather than an abrupt change. In 1965, the first generation of ESEA's Title I focused on providing compensatory services to educationally disadvantaged youth, often delivering these services outside the regular classroom. Expectations for program outcomes were vague, and, therefore, accountability measures were lax. Thus, the program operated at a distance from the governance and operation of public schools. In part due to the report "A Nation at Risk" (NCEE, 1983), the focus of the program shifted during the Reagan and G.H.W. Bush presidencies from delivery of services to achieve educational opportunity and equity to standards and outcomes— with the goals of educational excellence and greater student achievement (McDonnell, 2005). The second generation of Title I was heavily influenced by an educational reform movement calling for better articulation and measurement of the content and performance standards for what students should know and be able to do. These content standards are an accountability tool in their own right because they define at the state level the material that teachers are responsible for covering and students are responsible for mastering. Without a standard for what students must know at a given grade level, there can be no absolute target for "proficiency"; however, that construct is defined and measured. Thus, the concerns educators express about the excessive focus on accountability reflect a concern about the scope and depth of the material educators are expected to teach as much as the focus on summary statistics derived from standardized tests (Marzano, 2003; Popham, 2006).

The third generation of Title I emerged through the Clinton administration's reauthorization, Improving America's Schools Act (IASA). The net result of this iteration was to move federal education policy into the mainstream of local school operations through several key provisions: (1) the learning goals, expectations, and curriculum for Title I students were to be the same as for all other students; (2) states were required to submit plans and annual reports specifying curricular standards and assessment results; and (3) states were required to hold LEAs accountable for making adequate progress. Thus, when the G. W. Bush administration took office in 2001 the framework for standards and accountability reflected in NCLB had evolved through the previous 36 years of legislation and public policy. What fell to this next generation of Title I was to articulate a precise definition of goals for student proficiency (100%) and establish the timeline for annual yearly progress (by 2014) and the programs and the actions to be taken when schools consistently fail to meet their targets (McDonnell, 2005).

It is important for evaluators to be aware of several other areas of public policy that interact with implementation of NCLB. The federal Individuals with Disabilities Education Improvement Act of 2004 (IDEA, 2004) establishes provisions for educating children with disabilities. Many states have laws and regulations pertaining to education of English learners as well as a state-governed academic performance and accountability program that may vary somewhat from the NCLB program.

Standards and Assessment—The Precursors to Accountability

Assuming that states wish to receive federal Title I funding, they must adopt plans meeting the provisions defined in Title I, Part A, Subpart 1—section 1111, the source for this section as well as the following sections on AYP and AMOs (NCLB, 2001). Rigorous content standards, describing what elementary and secondary students must know and be able to do in the content areas of math, language arts and reading, and science are an essential ingredient of the plan. States must define "proficient" performance that constitutes the benchmark level of mastery that students are expected to attain, along with the rung above—("advanced") and the rung below ("basic," which some states have further divided into "basic," "below basic," and "far below basic").

This performance is measured through academic assessments geared to content standards. To determine yearly performance, NCLB called for states by 2005–2006 to administer annual assessments in reading and language arts and math, at a minimum, to all students in grade levels three through eight. The law spells out the minimum criteria that assessments must meet: (1) the same assessments must be used to measure the achievement of all children within each state—with accommodations and modifications for students with disabilities; (2) tests must be aligned with the state's challenging academic content standards; (3) tests must meet adequate professional testing standards for technical quality; (4) tests must involve multiple measures of higher order thinking skills; and (5) results must be disaggregated at the state, LEA, and school levels by gender and major demographic groups (see later discussion for definition of major groups). In addition to standardized assessments, states may also define other academic performance indicators, provided they are valid, reliable, apply to all public school students, and are measured for each demographic subgroup. These indicators may include factors such as additional state or local assessments, grade-to-grade retention rate, student attendance and percentage of students completing advanced placement courses, and gifted and talented programs or college preparatory courses. The mix of indicators for secondary school students must include the graduation rate, defined as the percentage of students who graduate with a regular diploma in the standard number of years.

The stipulations for assessment under NCLB did not specify that a single national test be used to hold states accountable for academic achievement; each state has its own standardized testing program. However, there is one test that is administered across multiple states that can be used as a basis for comparison. The National Assessment of Educational Progress (NAEP; U.S. Department of Education, 2006) is administered once every 2 years nationwide to students in the fourth and eighth grades in reading and mathematics (NAEP tests also exist for a variety of other content areas), and periodically to 12th graders. The NAEP is not used to gauge progress toward NCLB accountability requirements, but it can be used as a single national yardstick to compare the rigor of state assessments used for NCLB. Because much of education policy and practice has historically been left to the states, there are variations in the level of rigor in both the scope of content standards and the meaning of test results. A level of performance considered proficient in one state could be labeled one notch lower, or basic, in another. A recent report by the National Center for Education Statistics maps state proficiency standards to NAEP scales (U.S. Department of Education, 2007). The report demonstrates the tremendous variability among states in their expectation of the performance required to be considered proficient and thus the ease with which a state or its LEAs could achieve the targets described here.

Adequate Yearly Progress. State plans must specify what will constitute AYP for all public schools and LEAs to demonstrate that they meet the state's student academic achievement standards. In what is perhaps one of the most controversial aspects of NCLB, the law requires that states develop a timeline culminating with all students in each demographic group reaching or exceeding proficiency in both content areas (mathematics, reading and language arts) by the 2013–2014 school year. The intent is for every public school in the state to be held to the same standard of academic achievement, for achievement to be measured through statistically valid and reliable assessments, and for all students to make continuous and substantial progress toward the objective of 100% proficiency by 2013–2014 (and within specified demographic subgroups). The law is concerned with closing gaps in academic achievement among various demographic groups. Thus, there is a requirement that 95% of students enrolled in a school, including individuals with disabilities, must participate in the assessment program and any other indicators. Limited English proficiency (LEP) students are included in the assessments and reporting if they have resided in the United States for longer than a year. Separate measurable objectives and annual reporting are also required for economically disadvantaged students and students from major racial and ethnic groups. The demographic categories are not necessarily mutually exclusive; one student's assessment results could be counted within several groups. Data for one of these student categories are not reported if the number of students in the group is too small to yield statistically reliable information or the results would reveal personally identifiable information.

Annual Measurable Objectives. Schools and LEAs are required to meet a set of AMOs as a way of ensuring that progress is made toward the ultimate objective of 100% proficiency by 2013–2014. The states set these AMOs, although NCLB specifies the framework for what is required. The AMOs must include a requirement that 95% of students participate in testing in both content areas. Statewide AMOs are set for the percentage of students who are expected to be proficient in reading and language arts and mathematics. The AMOs for the percentage proficient in the two content areas ramp up over the years, starting with the state's baseline in 2001–2002 and progressing upward to 100% 12 years later. It was left to the states to determine how to allocate the slope over the years. For example, currently in California 35.2% of students should be at or above proficiency in English language arts in 2007–2008, and this increases to 56.8% by 2009–2010. Finally, the states determined AMOs for "other indicators." In the case of California, schools are required to demonstrate growth on a state calculated Academic Performance Index (API). The California API is a single composite that indicates a school's position relative to all other schools in the state as well as demographically similar schools. Annual growth targets are set using the previous year's baseline API. A school's growth is calculated by comparing the current year's API to the baseline API from the previous year. The API score is a composite of all the school's standardized test scores weighted for the relative importance of content areas (as an example, language arts gets a higher weight than science) and the number of students who took each test. High schools also have an AMO for improving their graduation rate. The AMOs for testing participation and proficiency in mathematics and reading and language arts applies to the student body as a whole as well as to each applicable demographic subgroup. As an example, a California high school with a diverse student population might have 22 or more separate AMOs. This would include AMOs for both test participation and percentage proficient for each of five demographic groups (such as schoolwide plus Hispanics, socioeconomically disadvantaged, English learners, and students with disabilities)—a total of 20 AMOs in all, plus an AMO for increasing their California API and one for improving the graduation rate. If the school meets the 22 AMOs, then it is considered to have demonstrated AYP. If the school falls short on any one of the AMOs, then it has not demonstrated AYP.

Consequences for Not Demonstrating Adequate Yearly Progress

If a school does not meet one of its AMOs for 2 consecutive years and thus does not demonstrate AYP, it moves into what is called program improvement (PI) status (NCLB, 2001, sect. 1116). During year 1 of PI, which is at the beginning of the third year following 2 years of not making AYP, schools must offer to parents, at LEA expense, transportation to another school in the district that has demonstrated AYP. Year 1 PI schools are entitled to technical assistance to address the issues that led to failure to demonstrate AYP. Using this technical assistance, schools should develop or revise 2-year school-improvement plans, incorporating research-based strategies among other things. In year 2 of PI, schools continue to receive technical assistance as well as offer supplemental educational services to students from low-income families. In PI year 3, LEAs are required to take corrective action, which might consist of replacing staff, implementing a new scientifically based curriculum, or imposing some other type of reorganization. In PI year 4, LEAs must develop a plan that may involve replacing staff, reopening the school as a charter school, or any other major restructuring. In year 5, the alternative governance plan developed in year 4 must be implemented.

Providing Resources to Meet the AYP Challenge

A public school is a complex organization to run, but simply stated, the ability of a school to effectively deliver its program to students depends, in large part, on the quality of the teaching staff, the teaching practices they employ, and the instructional materials available for their use. NCLB and its subsequent policy clarifications focused on two critical resources: educational tools and qualified teachers.

Scientifically Tested Educational Tools. NCLB calls for educators to use educational programs and instructional strategies that have been validated through SBR. The term is used frequently throughout NCLB, and DOE clarified its meaning several years later (U.S. Department of Education, 2005) in an announcement specifying that federal decisions to fund research investigating the effectiveness of education policies and program interventions would assign a priority to studies using random assignment or quasi-experimental research designs. In cases where ethical or feasibility issues limit options for random assignment of students, teachers, classrooms, or schools to treatment versus control conditions, quasi-experimental techniques can be used: carefully matched comparison groups, regression discontinuity, and single-subject designs using multiple baseline or treatment reversal or interrupted time series. In publishing this announcement, DOE noted that the priority was established "for projects proposing an evaluation plan. . . . to assess the effectiveness of a particular intervention" (U.S. Department of Education, 2005, p. 3586).

The ensuing controversy within the program evaluation field played out in several forums. The Spring 2007 issue of *New Directions for Evaluation* was devoted to a thorough review of the matter (Julnes & Rog, 2007). Writers on both sides of the issue appear to agree that the choice of an evaluation method should fit the evaluation question being investigated; but they seem to disagree as to the scope of the DOE priority (Chelimsky, 2007; Lipsey, 2007). In any case, at least when it comes to testing the effectiveness of educational interventions using federal funds, evaluators should be aware that as an NCLB policy decision DOE has established guidelines favoring evaluation methods that use experimental controls whenever feasible.

Researchers and practitioners looking for effective practices that have been scientifically validated according to DOE guidelines can turn to a federally supported repository known as the What Works Clearinghouse (WWC). Research reports on selected topics are included in the WWC only if they are based on a randomized control trial (RCT) experimental design or a quasi-experimental approach, such as equating, regression discontinuity, or single-case (repeated measure) designs. (Chapter 7 of this volume is a specific discussion of the impact of WWC requirements.) As of April 2007, the WWC included evidence-based reviews of practices in the areas of beginning reading, early childhood education, dropout prevention, elementary school math, English language learners, character education, and middle school math curriculum.

To assist educators in weighing the evidence, DOE has issued guidelines (U.S. Department of Education, 2003) to consider in determining whether educational interventions are, in fact, supported by rigorous evidence and might be successfully adopted in their context. Elements to consider in determining the strength of evidence supporting program effectiveness are use of RCTs in two or more school settings—(including a setting similar to the one considering adopting the program), clear descriptions of the training of those who implemented the program (such as certificated teacher vs. paraprofessional), the amount of training they received to deliver the intervention, the curriculum used, characteristics of the students involved in the study, the description of the control group and the intervention they received, the logic describing how the program produces its intended effect, and the use of valid measures that are sensitive to the program outcomes.

Qualified Staff. NCLB requires that state implementation plans ensure that teachers and paraprofessionals teaching in core academic subjects be highly qualified by the end of the 2005–2006 school year (NCLB, 2001, sect. 1119) and later revised to the end of the 2006–2007 school year (Thompson & Barnes, 2007). The definition of a highly qualified teacher comprises full state certification, holding a bachelor's degree, and passing a test demonstrating subject matter knowledge (NCLB, 2001, sect. 9101). Paraprofessionals are expected to have completed a 2-year associate degree along with passing a state assessment (NCLB, 2001, sect. 1119).

Proposed Reauthorization Changes

Congress began considering reauthorization of the NCLB legislation in 2007. A bipartisan, independent commission was formed to collect public testimony and recommend ways to improve the law (Thompson & Barnes, 2007). Here is a brief synopsis of the highlights of these recommendations:

- The highly qualified teacher requirements would be expanded to require that states develop data systems capable of tracking individual student progress over time in a way that measures a teacher's "value added" contribution to student learning
- Principals would be subject to quality standards for the first time, including a measure of their school's progress in improving student subgroup performance relative to other schools with comparable demographics
- The proportion of students in a district who can be assessed for AYP purposes using alternative assessments against alternative standards would increase from 1% to 2% for children with significant cognitive disabilities
- Growth factors would be added to the AYP model, allowing students to be considered proficient if the trend in their achievement results indicates that they are on track to reach proficiency within 3 years—a provision also requiring states to implement data systems capable of tracking longitudinal assessment results at the student level
- AMOs for science achievement would be added (a double-edged sword—a win for the sciences, coming with the requirement that 100% of students be proficient by 2013–2014 with a much shorter ramp-up period
- Evaluations of supplemental educational services, such as tutoring provided to students in schools not making AYP, would be launched
- The research and development budget for SBR would be doubled

In addition to NCLB commission recommendations, state education officials and other education interest groups will undoubtedly argue for greater flexibility in NCLB for schools that have demonstrated measurable progress in student achievement but today are categorized as PI. The alternative is that states with the most rigorous standards will also be most likely to have nearly all of their schools and districts labeled as program improvement by 2013–2014. According to California Superintendent

New Directions for Evaluation • DOI: 10.1002/ev

of Public Instruction Jack O'Connell (2007), "There must be a way of differentiating a school or a district that is truly struggling with one that is clearly on the right track" (p. 1). In no scenario, though, does it appear that the nation's long march toward school accountability and performance management will waver. No political figure will want to establish an accountability standard that guarantees the existence of a certain margin of failure; nor will the nation's educators want to back away from closing the achievement gap between poor or minority students and the rest of the country.

Conclusion

The federal accountability requirements for public education have evolved over a 40-year period. At the inception of Title I in 1965, the federal government stood at arm's length from state and local school district governance and operations. Title I funded a well-intentioned, but loosely defined, set of services for educationally disadvantaged youth operating primarily outside the regular classroom. Today, federal mandates for educational accountability and educational evaluation are positioned front and center among the core factors driving most public school districts and educational evaluations. Far from being imposed by an unsympathetic political faction within a short period of time, the evolution as described here occurred with the involvement of educators, academic theorists, state governors, business leaders, and a broad bipartisan base of legislators (Mathison, 2005; McDonnell, 2005). Policy makers may tinker with various provisions in subsequent revisions to ESEA/NCLB, but it is unlikely that the foundation, once erected, will quickly be dismantled. Within the field of program evaluation, some leaders believe that provisions favoring controlled experimentation merely bring the educational enterprise to the same degree of rigorous evidence base that other fields, such as medicine, have long taken for granted (Slavin, 2002). Other investigators argue that other methodological approaches are capable of producing equally valid, actionable conclusions (Chelimsky, 2007). Observers from all camps would probably agree that we have a long way to go before researchers produce the educational equivalent of a scientifically based drug formulary of programs and program components that practitioners can pull off the shelf to close the achievement gap.

References

Boruch, R. (2007). Encouraging the flight of error: Ethical standards, evidence standards, and randomized trials. *New Directions for Evaluation, 113,* 55–73.
Center on Education Policy. (2007). *No Child Left Behind at five: A review of change to state accountability plans.* Washington, DC: Center on Education Policy.

Chelimsky, E. (2007). Factors influencing the choice of methods in federal evaluation practice. In G. Julnes & D. Rog (Eds.), *Informing federal policies on evaluation methodology: Building the evidence base for method choice in government sponsored evaluation. New Directions for Evaluation, 113,* 13–33.

Donaldson, S. I., Christie, C. A., & Mark, M. M. (in press). *What counts as credible evidence in applied research and contemporary evaluation practice?* Newbury Park, CA: Sage.

EdSource. (2007). *Resource cards on California schools.* Mountain View, CA: Author.

Individuals with Disabilities Education Act of 2004, Public Law No. 108–446.

Julnes, G., & Rog, D. J. (2007). Informing federal policies on evaluation methodology: Building the evidence base for method choice in government sponsored evaluation. *New Directions for Evaluation, 113.*

Lipsey, M. W. (2007). Method choice for government evaluation: The beam in our own eye. In G. Julnes & D. Rog (Eds.), *Informing federal policies on evaluation methodology: Building the evidence base for method choice in government sponsored evaluation. New Directions for Evaluation, 113,* 113–115.

Marzano, R. J. (2003). *What works in schools: Translating research into action.* Alexandria, VA: Association for Supervision and Curriculum Development.

Mathison, S. (2005, August). *Public good and private interest in educational evaluation.* Paper presented at meeting of American Psychological Association, Washington, DC. Retrieved September 24, 2007, from http://web.mac.com/sandra.mathison/iWeb/writing/other%20jottings_files/Educational%20Evaluation.pdf

McDonnell, L. M. (2005). No Child Left Behind and the federal role in education: Evolution or revolution? *Peabody Journal of Education, 80,* 19–38.

National Commission on Educational Excellence. (1983). *A nation at risk: The imperative for educational reform.* Washington, DC: U.S. Government Printing Office.

No Child Left Behind Act. (2001). Public Law No. 107–110. 107th Congress, 110 *Congressional Record* 1425, 115 Stat.

O'Connell, J. (2007). *Schools chief Jack O'Connell responds to President Bush's proposed revisions to No Child Left Behind act.* Retrieved June 6, 2007, from http://www.cde.ca.gov/nr/ne/yr07/yr07rel19.asp

Popham, W. J. (2006). Content standards: The unindicted co-conspirator. *Educational Leadership, 64,* 87–88.

Slavin, R. E. (2002). Evidence-based education policies: Transforming educational practice and research. *Educational Researcher, 31,* 15–21.

Smith, E. (2005). Raising standards in American schools: The case of No Child Left Behind. *Journal of Education Policy, 20,* 507–524.

Thompson, T. G., & Barnes, R. E. (2007). *Beyond NCLB: Fulfilling the promise to our nation's children.* Report of the commission on No Child Left Behind. Washington, DC: Aspen Institute.

U.S. Department of Education. (2002). *Stronger accountability: Key policy letters signed by the education secretary or deputy secretary.* Retrieved April 14, 2007, from http://www.ed.gov/policy/elsec/guid/secletter/020724.html

U.S. Department of Education. (2003). *Identifying and implementing educational practices supported by rigorous evidence: A user friendly guide.* Washington, DC: U.S. Department of Education, Institute of Education Sciences, National Center for Education Evaluation and Regional Assistance.

U.S. Department of Education. (2005). Scientifically based evaluation methods (RIN 1890-ZA00). *Federal Register, 70*(15), 3586–3589.

U.S. Department of Education. (2006). *The nation's report card: Reading 2005.* Washington, DC: U.S. Department of Education, National Center for Educational Statistics.

U.S. Department of Education. (2007). *Mapping 2005 state proficiency standards onto the NAEP scales.* Washington, DC: U.S. Department of Education, National Center for Educational Statistics.

West, M. R. (2005). *No Child Left Behind: How to give it a passing grade* (Policy Brief no. 149.) Washington, DC: Brookings Institution Press.

W. K. Kellogg Foundation. (1998). *Evaluation handbook*. Battle Creek, MI: Author.

JACK I. MILLS *is a practicing local educational evaluator in Claremont, California; he was formerly on the school governing board of the Claremont Unified School District.*

NEW DIRECTIONS FOR EVALUATION • DOI: 10.1002/ev

Mabry, L. (2008). Consequences of No Child Left Behind on evaluation purpose, design, and impact. In T. Berry & R. M. Eddy (Eds.), *Consequences of No Child Left Behind for educational evaluation. New Directions for Evaluation, 117,* 21–36.

2

Consequences of No Child Left Behind on Evaluation Purpose, Design, and Impact

Linda Mabry

Abstract

As an outgrowth of No Child Left Behind's narrow definition of scientifically based research, the priority given to certain quantitative evaluation designs has sparked debate among those in the evaluation community. Federal mandates for particular evaluation methodologies run counter to evaluation practice and to the direction of most evaluation theorists, who advocate for flexibility and adaptability in methods choices. The impact of this mandate for randomized clinical trials as the sine qua non of evaluation methods is not yet discernible, but the potential impact is explored through an analogous example involving the World Bank. © Wiley Periodicals, Inc.

O n November 4, 2003, the U.S. Department of Education (DOE) proposed "a priority for program projects [using] an evaluation plan that is based on rigorous scientifically based research methods to assess the effectiveness of a particular intervention . . . in accordance with the Elementary and Secondary Education Act (ESEA) as reauthorized by the *No Child Left Behind* Act of 2001" (NCLB, 2001), declaring:

NEW DIRECTIONS FOR EVALUATION, no. 117, Spring 2008 © Wiley Periodicals, Inc.
Published online in Wiley InterScience (www.interscience.wiley.com) • DOI: 10.1002/ev.249

> Evaluation methods using an experimental design are best for determining project effectiveness. . . . If random assignment is not feasible, the project may use a quasi-experimental design with carefully matched comparison conditions. . . . For projects that are focused on special populations in which sufficient numbers of participants are not available to support random assignment or matched comparison group designs, single-subject designs such as multiple baseline or treatment-reversal or interrupted time series that are capable of demonstrating causal relationships can be employed. . . . Proposed evaluation strategies that use neither *experimental designs* with random assignment nor *quasi-experimental designs* using a matched comparison group nor *regression discontinuity designs* will not be considered responsive to the priority when sufficient numbers of participants are available to support these designs. (DOE, 2003, p. 62446)

Over vigorous objection from professionals within the evaluation community, including an official response that stirred intense internal controversy within the American Evaluation Association (AEA), the DOE announced its intention to establish the so-called gold, silver, and bronze standards in funding education projects requiring evaluation of outcomes. The proposal mirrored an earlier DOE priority for funding research that prompted similarly vigorous response from educational researchers (see Berliner, 2002; Eisenhart & Towne, 2003; Erickson, & Gutierrez, 2002; Feuer, Towne, & Shavelson, 2002; Pellegrino & Goldman, 2002; Viadero, 2006, 2007).

Among evaluators, the proposal for the funding priority reignited long dormant "paradigm wars" (Datta, 1994; Guba, 1990) over the relative merits of quantitative and qualitative methodology and raised concerns that the new policy would "discourage a *repertoire of methods* [and] would force evaluators backward" (AEA, 2003). Also at risk, thought some evaluators, was attention to program process, contexts, formative feedback, and ethical treatment of program participants. The impact—or likely impact—of the DOE priority on educational evaluation is the subject of this text.

Regulation of Methods

The DOE justified its preferential priority, which went into effect in February 2005, on the basis of scientific rigor:

> We take this action to focus Federal financial assistance on expanding the number of programs and projects Department-wide that are evaluated under rigorous scientifically based research methods in accordance with the Elementary and Secondary Education Act of 1965 (ESEA), as reauthorized by the *No Child Left Behind* Act of 2001 (NCLB) . . . the Secretary considers random assignment and quasi-experimental designs to be the most rigorous to address the question of project effectiveness. (DOE, 2005, p. 3586)

Even the DOE's proposal to prioritize certain design types sounded alarms in the evaluation community. Because the proposal was made public through the *Federal Register* as the AEA convened its annual week-long conference and because the opportunity to respond to the proposal was open for only a month, some evaluators questioned whether the DOE had timed its announcement to limit replies from practicing evaluators attending the meeting of their professional organization. In the short period available, the AEA Board of Directors' Executive Committee[1] established a task force[2] to draft a response for the association[3], approved the draft response with no change of wording, issued the response, and distributed it electronically to AEA members while encouraging individual member responses as well.

The AEA response to the DOE's invitation to comment was among nearly 300 received, the vast majority in agreement with the AEA statement. For example, 183 respondents explained that the prioritized designs were not the only ones capable of indicating causality, 173 that experimental and quasi-experimental design limited investigation to a small number of isolated factors, 186 that such designs could violate ethical standards when used in education, 174 that many educational programs are too small for such designs, and 242 that the evaluation purpose or question should determine the methods. Although only 29 respondents supported the proposed priority (DOE, 2005, pp. 3588–3589), the DOE ultimately "determined that the comments did not warrant changes" (p. 3586).

Debate regarding the role of government in determining evaluation methods, catalyzed by the proposed priority, has continued beyond its establishment. On one side, the arguments claim that "there is little evidence of federal agencies promoting any method as a one-size-fits-all approach to program evaluation. The place one is likely to find such overblown claims is among evaluators themselves" (Lipsey, 2007, p. 115). On the other side are arguments that the DOE's priority "makes no sense in the thoughtful development of an evaluation design" (Chelimsky, 2007, p. 31).

Dissensus

Disagreements regarding appropriate methodology in research and evaluation have recurred over the past quarter century. As qualitative researchers struggled to achieve credibility for their interpretive, ethnographic, phenomenological inquiries within a publication context favoring quantitative studies, the positions on each side were characterized as incommensurable (Lincoln & Guba, 1985). In evaluation, where a dozen or so distinct evaluation approaches (sometimes called models) demonstrate some of the methodological diversity among evaluators (Madaus, Scriven, & Stufflebeam, 1987; Stufflebeam, 2001; Worthen, Sanders, & Fitzpatrick, 1997), debate was sometimes heated (e.g., Miller & Campbell, 2006; Scriven, 1972; Stufflebeam, 1994; Stufflebeam et al., 2001). Questions surfaced regarding accuracy and utility, two program evaluation standards (Joint Committee, 1994). The AEA's refusal to license or certify evaluators, despite repeated suggestions that this might encourage or improve competence in practice, suggests, in part, wariness of methodological schisms and their potential for further controversy and politicization.

Over time, "there has been no shortage of serious efforts to reconcile opposing views on proper approaches to evaluation" (Julnes & Rog, 2007a, p. 1). The emergence of mixed methods (Greene & Caracelli, 1997; Greene, Caracelli, & Graham, 1989; see also Chatterji, 2004; Johnson & Onwuegbuzie, 2004; Mertens, 2005) offered one way to bridge the gap in a declared truce (House, 1994), although the mix in mixed methods was sometimes more lopsided in practice than in theory. As the controversy ebbed and flowed, there have been reminders that evaluators agree about the importance of accessibility to an array of methodological approaches and the inadvisability of narrow options, for example: "Proclaiming almost any single design as the best in any or all program contexts, without adequate attention to what is happening in the real world, is unlikely to be wise, a thought that is almost an evaluation cliché" (Datta, 2007, p. 50).

Sometimes, an "affirmation of incommensurates" (Lather, 1993, p. 687) has been discernible, for example, in the admission that "even scientists with strong preferences for randomized experiments also acknowledge that other research designs can often yield useful information" (Shadish & Rindskopf, 2007, p. 96). Shifting the ground of the evolving debate, the DOE priority for funding a small group of methodological approaches introduced governmental regulation into the practice of evaluation.

Methods in Use

In the Federal Government. Because of its relative newness, it remains to be seen whether the DOE priority will result in long-term negative consequences to methodological diversity in federally funded evaluations in education, and if so, whether constrained evaluation practice will have an impact on federally sponsored education programs, evaluation practice outside the DOE, or continued development of evaluation approaches and refinements. Not only without, but also within, the governmental context, policy impact remains difficult to determine because "no group [is] systematically monitoring federal legislation, grant announcements, or Requests for Proposals to describe the range of approaches to evaluation design and assess their appropriateness" (Datta, 2007, p. 51).

Acknowledging these caveats, Lois-ellin Datta (2007) examined designs used for evaluations commissioned by federal agencies over the past 15 years, GAO reports on government evaluations, some government regulations, evaluation reports, and other types of documentation related to federally sponsored evaluations, finding:

New Directions for Evaluation • DOI: 10.1002/ev

- The Office of Management and Budget (OMB), whose "judgments affect all federal agencies" (p. 41), has shown preference for random assignment design and for logic models showing causal relationships among program elements.
- "The National Institutes of Health (NIH) regard randomized designs as the standard . . . preferably double-blind" (p. 40).
- "Project Head Start is also among agencies conducting primarily randomized design studies" (p. 40).
- The Substance Abuse and Mental Health Services Administration (SAMHSA) allows reviewers to award proposals "an extra 20 points if the design involves a randomized control group" (p. 40).
- The Bureau of Indian Affairs (BIA) "has encouraged ethnographic approaches" (p. 42) over a long period of time because of the importance of culture in its programs.
- The Department of Justice has prominently employed "case study evaluations and case study research" (p. 43), perhaps unsurprisingly given the case-based nature of its function.
- The National Science Foundation (NSF) has demonstrated "interest in methodological diversity and exploration" (p. 44).
- The Government Accounting Office's (GAO) work in synthesizing published studies favored inquiries that used experimental designs but, "for its own studies, GAO has applied a perhaps exceptionally wide range of evaluation designs" (p. 40).

In the decade and a half that Eleanor Chelimsky served as head of the GAO's Program and Evaluation and Methodology Division (the pioneer of the evaluation synthesis method), meta-analysis of prior studies resulted in "a new appreciation and use for the experimental evaluations that had been performed in the past" (p. 20). In their own data collection, GAO personnel weighed methodological pros and cons and regarded access to an array of methodological options as critical. For example, Chelimsky (2007) stated: "Flexibility in methods choice and serious consideration of alternative design options are not luxuries [but rather a responsibility that] has traditionally belonged to the evaluator. It is that responsibility that undergirds evaluative credibility" (p. 31).

Matching methods to each evaluation to be performed, GAO personnel found:

> Experimental design is of great value when a cause-and-effect question must be answered because of its special ability to make causal inferences, but it usually requires the help of other methods to make it viable. And since the majority of questions asked in federally sponsored evaluations are not cause-and-effect questions, the experimental design is often irrelevant. (p. 23)

Although "some work has been done . . . with studies and meta-analyses that seek to demonstrate relationships between different methodologies and the resulting impact estimates," this work has rarely examined "how different methodologies produce findings that are useful and used to guide action" (Julnes & Rog, 2007a, p. 4). One such examination, Howell and Yemane's review of evaluations (2006) for 12 large, multisite federal projects found only two had used randomized experimental and control groups, and that in general the studies failed to yield adequate outcome data or analyses and also did not justify the cost, a total of $115 million.

In education, from her vantage point as former national director of Head Start Evaluation, Datta recalled congressional imposition of randomized experimental methods on a study of Head Start's effectiveness in developing the academic skills of impoverished children as "a horrific example of the inappropriate use of what can be, in appropriate circumstances, an excellent design" (2007, p. 49), its effect having been "closer to homicide than to evaluation" (p. 48). In sum, efforts to review evaluations of federally sponsored programs indicate that some, but not all, U.S. government agencies favor experimental designs, and among those that do, such designs have not always proved beneficial.

In an Analogous Context: The World Bank Evaluation Priority. Because it may be too early to detect the effect that the federal priority regarding evaluation methods exerts on evaluation practice, an analogy may be helpful in securing predictive insight. Because an analogy is never identical to the case in point, caution is in order, akin to the idea that although history rarely, if ever, repeats itself exactly, it often rhymes. In this case, the analogy to the DOE's methodological priority involves another large administrative body with a history of somewhat similar methodological preferences in the evaluations it sponsors: the World Bank.

Established at the end of World War II along with the International Monetary Fund (IMF), the World Bank is owned by more than 180 shareholding member countries. The bank initiated projects in education in 1962, and by 2006 it had become the largest provider of external funding for education in the world, with approximately 200 education staff members of whom about a fifth had graduate training in education (Alexander, 1998). Based on the idea that "investment in education can contribute to economic growth" (Psacharopoulos & Woodhall, 1991, p. 21), five principles underlying the Bank's educational investment strategy have been articulated:

1. Basic education should be provided for all children and adults.
2. To increase productivity and promote social equity, educational opportunities should be provided without distinction of sex, ethnic background, or social and economic status.
3. Education systems should try to achieve maximum internal efficiency.
4. Education should be related to work.
5. Developing countries will need to build and maintain their institutional capacity to design, analyze, manage, and evaluate programs for education and training (p. 5).

New Directions for Evaluation • DOI: 10.1002/ev

For the Bank, "an investment is considered profitable . . . when the expected benefits exceed its costs" (p. 29). But focusing on "economic analysis of investment choices" (Psacharopoulos & Woodhall, 1991, p. 10) limits the Bank's view of education to an economic one—a "stark contrast with such other agencies as UNESCO, whose educational concerns remain conceptually broad" (Jones, 1992, p. 224).

The Bank's narrow perspective has led to a "clearly defined methodological orientation" (Jones, 1992, p. 228) in evaluating its educational projects, one that prioritizes experimental designs with randomized groups, as the U.S. Department of Education now also does. The Bank offers this justification for its evaluation priority: "Impact evaluation is a policy tool that helps discern the causal impact of a project or a policy initiative. . . . Conceptually, impact evaluation seeks to estimate the effect of a given intervention on an important development indicator by comparing with and without the intervention on the same unit of observation" (World Bank, 2007).

A general view of this methodological preference, however, summarized as follows, reduces the Bank's justification to a mere claim:

> Objectives-based evaluation gained increasing consideration by professionals during the 1960s and early 1970s, but criticism of this evaluation approach soon emerged. Indeed, objectives-based evaluation came under much scrutiny and condemnation. . . . Critics argue that because emphasis is on the measure of objectives (rather than on judging the merit of the program), objectives-based evaluation does not have a true evaluation component. . . . The World Bank's Operations Evaluation Department uses an objectives-based evaluation approach to evaluate development work. The World Bank claims that this approach to evaluating its work has three important advantages: It enhances accountability, promotes efficiency, and allows comparisons. (Christie & Alkin, 2005, p. 284)

Despite the unflattering history of the Bank's methods, it has persisted in pursuing econometric correlations linking education and economic productivity through "cost-benefit analysis, cost-effectiveness analysis, and the analysis of demand for and utilization of manpower" (Psacharopoulos & Woodhall, 1991, p. 24). In doing so, it has neglected "just what it is about education that makes people actually or potentially more productive, and [as a result of] which types of education" (Jones, 1992, p. 235); the processes "central to a broader and deeper understanding of education" (p. 230); and "detailed audits seeking reasonable assurance that funds disbursed have been applied as intended" (p. xv). By its own reckoning, the Bank has even neglected student learning: "Only about one in five projects had an explicit objective to improve student learning" (World Bank Independent Evaluation Group, IEG, 2006, p. xv). An evaluation of its approach to education surfaced a significant caution related to the DOE priority for evaluation methods similar to those of the Bank: "Focus on quantitative growth can overshadow improvements in educational quality and outcomes, including student learning outcomes" (p. 26).

This lack of focus has been compounded by the Bank's operational definitions, which have been economically rather than educationally oriented; as an example, "The term *'quality'* has been used synonymously with the *'internal efficiency'* of education, a material and focused concern of the economics of education" (Jones, 1992, p. 257). Its criteria for evaluating impact have also been defined economically: "Economic evaluation of educational investment projects should take into account the following *criteria*: Direct economic returns to investment . . . indirect economic returns . . . fiscal benefits in the form of higher taxes paid . . . satisfaction of demand for skilled manpower . . . the private demand for education . . . internal efficiency of educational institutions" . . . (Psacharopoulos & Woodhall, 1991, p. 26).

As with NCLB, World Bank evaluations take test scores as a key indicator of the success of an educational program. Because of the emphasis on this indicator of educational impact, since 1990 the Bank has allocated funds toward development of national assessments and indicator systems focused on test scores (IEG, 2006). With these assessment and indicator systems in place, its evaluations have used test scores to determine, for example, whether use of textbooks or wall charts improves the test scores of Kenyan children (Glewwe, Kremer, & Moulin, 2001; Glewwe, Kremer, Moulin, & Zitzewitz, 2004) or whether vouchers in Colombia are cost-effective (Angrist, Bettinger, Bloom, King, & Kremer, 2002).

Something is missing from the picture of education that such constrained evaluation can draw, according to the Bank itself: "More, better, and more contextualized analytic work is needed on learning outcomes and their determinants" (IEG, 2006, p. xvi). Incentives, perhaps unintended, have contributed to the "neglect of formative, qualitative project evaluation" (Jones, 1992, p. 266) as bank officers are rewarded for "negotiating large numbers of sizeable loans and in encouraging quick disbursements" (p. 220). In this big-money, high-speed context, ". . . troublesome data from qualitative evaluations can only slow down the process, an effect inimical to the careers of loan officers. In brief, the Bank displays no commitment whatever to monitoring the quality of project implementation for the purpose of correcting deficiencies for the remainder of the project" (p. 188).

"Areas of difficulty emerge when the Bank seeks to give the impression that its view of education is a comprehensive one," Jones (1992, p. 258) argues, because "such generality is dangerous and bears serious implications for borrowers" (p. 235). The implications to borrowers between 1963 and 1978 included "chronic failures in implementation strategies, the inadequacy of specialized facilities, the absence of appropriate instructional materials, unfamiliarity of curriculum objectives and principles, and above all the shortage of trained teachers [combining] to bring . . . devastating conclusions" (p. 253).

In the 1980s, ". . . the Bank failed to respect borrower differences [and reduced the] critical issues facing world education to five. . . . It became increasingly clear for which patterns and priorities financing would be made available. The weaker a borrower's economy, the less it was in a position to resist Bank formulations" (p. 223).

From the late 1980s, as a condition of awarding loans, the Bank promoted user fees in order for people in borrower countries to access health services and education (U.S. Network for Global Economic Justice, n.d.). By 1990, "subsidization of private schools [had] increased to questionable levels . . . in clear danger of jeopardizing public commitments to educational quality" (Jones, 1992, p. 249). In 2006, member nations of the Bank objected to loan conditions that "have a harmful impact on poor people, increasing their poverty not reducing it, by denying them access to vital services" (Kovach & Lansman, 2006, p. 3). "The Norwegian government [hosted] a conference on conditionality [and] commissioned research on the impact of conditions. Case study countries are Bangladesh, Mozambique, Zambia and Uganda. Preliminary findings include . . . pressure to privatize through the use of conditions" (Bretton Woods Project, 2006; see also Kovach & Lansman, 2006).

The Bank's Independent Evaluation Group (2006) painted a dismal picture of overall Bank impact in education, finding "few instances of improved learning outcomes among the disadvantaged" (p. 34). Given the connections among the Bank's investment strategies, evaluation strategies, and educational strategies, it would be hard to deny that the Bank's priority on evaluation methods, like that of the U.S. Department of Education, contributed to the tragic situation described by the Bank's own evaluation group: "Tens of millions of children in the developing world—primarily girls, the poor, and other disadvantaged groups—remain out of school; hundreds of millions drop out before completing primary school, and of those who do complete it, a large proportion fail to acquire desired levels of knowledge and skills, especially in the poorest countries" (IEG, 2006, p. xiii).

For the most part, the Bank has defended its approach, drawing on utilitarian ethics—the idea that "actions are right in proportion as they tend to promote [general] happiness" (Mill, 1863/1891, p. 9)—to argue: "The justification for any investment must be that it will make the greatest possible contribution. . . . This means that investment choices must be based both on cost-benefit analysis, which is concerned with external efficiency, and on cost-effectiveness analysis, which measures internal efficiency" (Psacharopoulos & Woodhall, 1991, p. 23).

From this perspective, "some opportunities have to be sacrificed when investment decisions are finally made" (p. 22), but surely sacrifice of public education (or access to it) is questionable on any ethical grounds. The Bank's jeopardizing of access to public education and promotion of privatized education mirror "conspiracy theories" increasingly vocalized in the United States in describing NCLB provisions regarding closure of public schools on the basis of test scores.

Clearly, Bank projects have affected education in developing countries, and the Bank's constrained evaluations have contributed to the effects. Evaluation practice outside the Bank may also be influenced by the general availability of Bank publications regarding methods (see, for example, Baker, 2000; Ravallion, 2006) and its increased visibility at professional evaluation meetings. It may be that the DOE priority regarding evaluation methods also has effects outside government. To date, the debate rekindled by the DOE priorities has led some researchers and evaluators to associate themselves explicitly and publicly with the methods preferred by the DOE (Viadero, 2006).

Comparison and Caution. The World Bank analogy shows how a methodological preference can limit evaluations and, because evaluations themselves affect programs, undermine educational programs. The Bank's preference for quantitative designs led to diversion of educational funds into development of quantitative indicators (test scores); likewise, the DOE has expressed preference for quantitative designs and, through NCLB, has caused diversion of federal and state funds into test-driven accountability systems and information management systems focused on test scores, a move some states have resisted.

In borrower countries, the Bank's loan conditions have limited access to public schools and promoted privatization of education. In the United States, NCLB sanctions have begun to result in public school closings; corporation-run charter schools have sometimes taken over, usually not performing as well as the public schools they replace (Schemo, 2004). If the World Bank is contributing to the marginalization or demise of public education in the developing world, partly through its preference for quantitative evaluation methods, is this what the United States faces as a result of the DOE's similar evaluation preference, a preference flowing from the legal mandate of NCLB?

Conclusion

If, as suggested earlier, evaluation is moving toward embrace of dissensus, it may be appropriate to offer in closing a vignette from personal practice, in accordance with postmodern insistence on individual truth. The experience related here, still ongoing, began in 2003, coincident with the DOE's proposal of its evaluation priority, and suggests ambiguity in the short-term impact of the policy on evaluation practice.

I had heard *sotto voce* reports that, because of the AEA's response to the proposed federal evaluation priority, government pressure was exerted on some members working in the context of federal agencies. Having chaired the AEA task force and having been named in the AEA's press releases (see http://www.eval.org/doepage.htm), I worried that my potential clients might be denied DOE funding if I were listed as their external evaluator. Three months before release of the AEA statement, a current client, a school district, won DOE funding in the Smaller Learning Communities (SLC) grant category established as part of federal implementation of NCLB, and I was about to begin an evaluation of the district's program in its four large high schools. The evaluation was designed to provide formative feedback in early years of implementation and summative information on program impact in a comprehensive report at the close of the final year.

As the first year of the evaluation drew to a close, the client notified me that the DOE required our joint attendance at a 3-day evaluation training workshop. We attended the workshop, sponsored by the Office of Vocational and Adult Education (OVAE) of the DOE, where we met personnel from the Northwest Regional Educational Laboratory (NWREL). When I asked workshop presenters from "DTI" what the initials stood for, they said, "Nothing"; when I pressed further, one replied, "defense technology industries." While I was wondering about the connection between the DOE and the Department of Defense, I asked about NWREL's role. Three NWREL staff members said they did not know; a fourth responded that they were to lend "technical assistance" to grantees.

Our formative first-year evaluation report was furnished to NWREL early in year 2, prior to its 2-day site visit, "to gather information about Smaller Learning Communities (SLC) program implementation and provide feedback to project schools to help them implement their SLC grants" (NWREL, 2004, p. 3). Prior to the site visit, my client was sent detailed evaluative rubrics to guide a self-study to be made available to the site-visit team; evidence on specified criteria was to be "gathered to assess progress" (p. 6). Program personnel focus shifted toward these unforeseen criteria, and the site visit was treated as a second external evaluation, despite NWREL insistence that it was "not intended as a summative program evaluation. . . . Rather, it is a critical-friend review that can produce new insights for the leadership team as it plans the next steps" (McGary-Hamilton & Luers, 2004, p. 2).

During the site-visit team's interview with me, I asked about a finding they informally reported to the project director, that literacy instruction was not rigorous. I was told that a single student in a group interview had so stated during their half-day visits to two of the four schools. When I asked what technical assistance my client could anticipate, the site visitors stammered that they would send a couple of NWREL documents for program personnel to read.

Because our data were collected using a mixed-methods design with qualitative emphasis, clearly lacking either a randomly selected or a matched control group, I expected censure in the NWREL report. Instead, our "excellent outside evaluation and rich data to inform implementation" (McGary-Hamilton & Luers, 2004, p. 5) were praised, the client was told informally that ours was the best SLC evaluation report in the region, and, some months later, the DOE requested our assistance with evaluation training for a new group of SLC awardees in California. Late in the third year of the evaluation, the DOE contacted me requesting permission to excerpt sections of the annual evaluation reports in their training materials—without credit or citation.

I consider the evaluation a case study, a design not favored by the DOE and once notoriously described as having "such a total absence of control as to be of almost no scientific value" (Campbell & Stanley, 1963, p. 6) but recently judged favorably, even for making causal inferences or for studying comprehensive educational reform initiatives (Shadish & Rindskopf, 2007; Yin & Davis, 2007). My methods could "not be considered responsive to the priority" (DOE, 2003) but yielded results repeatedly described by DOE representatives as exemplary. Such ambiguity raises questions:

- Will the DOE really support *appropriate evaluation methods* tailored to individual instances (for example, the priority "recognized that even for impact questions, other designs might be justified as more appropriate in some circumstances"; Lipsey, 2007, p. 114)?
- Is the DOE priority justifiable as a strategy to redress a *perceived methodological imbalance* ("Some feel that the current distribution of methods employed in federally sponsored evaluation is unbalanced because of too few random assignment experiments, and others feel that there is an imbalance due to the overemphasis given to randomized experiments"; Julnes & Rog, 2007b, p. 129)?
- Will the DOE priority continue the trend of awarding lucrative contracts to quantitative evaluators, with less lavishly financed, but more frequent, evaluations by qualitative practitioners ("The quants get the big evaluation contracts"; Rossi, 1994, p. 25)?

As for general issues for evaluation practice:

- Will the DOE priority affect, subtly or blatantly, the practice of evaluation in other government entities—or in nongovernmental settings?
- Will the DOE priority indirectly nudge theoretical understandings, individual tacit knowledge (Polanyi, 1958), or communal wisdom of practice about the meaning of competence in evaluation toward the gold, silver, and bronze standards—or away from them by spurring resistance?
- Will the discussion provoked among evaluators by the DOE priority promote alertness to its possible direct and indirect effects on practice? Will it clarify and solidify irreconcilable differences among evaluators, or encourage deeper appreciation of diverse methods?

NCLB insistence on scientifically based research and evaluation, narrowly construed, suggests its view of evaluation as a modernist practice—rational in its commitment to understanding reality through data, in its approach to improving programs and society through social science, and in its certainty that knowledge of programs confers power to readers of evaluation reports (see Mabry, 2002). But over the years, educational evaluation has grown in postmodern appreciation of diverse stakeholders, cultural contexts, and their power to shape program realities. It is possible that the evaluation profession's ultimate response to the DOE priority will be deepened appreciation for methodological diversity. Such an outcome may preclude consensus, inviting conflict and contradiction; it may also help evaluators deconstruct (Derrida, 1976) how experiences and proclivities channel vision and interpretation, and encourage us in the ongoing struggle to understand more fully and practice more sensitively.

Notes

1. The executive committee at that time was chaired by Richard Krueger, president of the AEA Board of Directors. Those invited to participate in the conference call included current officers of the board and newly elected officers who would assume responsibility the following January (2004): Nick Smith, president-elect; Molly Engle, past president; Sharon Rallis, future president; Nanette Keiser, treasurer; and Kathleen Bolland, treasurer-elect.

2. Task force members: Randall Davies, Ernest House, Cheri Levenson, Linda Mabry (chair), Sandra Mathison, Michael Scriven; reactors: Lois-ellin Datta, Burt Perrin, Katherine Ryan, Bob Williams. At that time, the chair of the AEA Public Affairs Committee, Jennifer Dewey, was encouraging an informal electronic mail discussion group of quantitatively oriented AEA members to draft an AEA public statement on randomized control trials, still controversial since the DoE's establishment of the gold, silver, and bronze standards in research about a year and a half earlier. All members of this discussion group were invited to join the task force, and all declined.

3. The proposal and priority as well as the AEA statement and press release can be found at http://www.eval.org/doepage.htm.

References

Alexander, N. C. (1998). *Paying for education: How the World Bank and IMF influence education in developing countries*. Report prepared for Oxfam America [mimeo].

American Evaluation Association. (2003). Response to U. S. Department of Education notice of proposed priority, "Scientifically Based Evaluation Methods" (*Federal Register* RIN 1890-ZA00). Retrieved November 4, 2003, from http://www.eval.org/doepage.htm

Angrist, J. D., Bettinger, E., Bloom, E., King, E., & Kremer, M. (2002). Vouchers for private schooling in Colombia: Evidence from a randomized natural experiment. *American Economic Review, 92,* 1535–1558.

Baker, J. (2000). *Evaluating the impact of development projects on poverty: A handbook for practitioners*. Washington, DC: World Bank.

Berliner, D. C. (2002). Educational research: The hardest science of all. *Educational Researcher, 31*(8), 18–20.

Bretton Woods Project: Critical voices on the World Bank and IMF. (2006). *Split highlights growing call to rethink conditionality*. New York: Global Policy Forum. Retrieved November 23, 2006, from http://www.globalpolicy.org/socecon/bwi-wto/wbank/2006/1123conditionality.htm

Campbell, D. T., & Stanley, J. C. (1963). *Experimental and quasi-experimental designs for research*. Boston: Houghton-Mifflin.

Chatterji, M. (2004). Evidence on "what works": An argument for extended-term mixed-method (ETMM) evaluation designs. *Educational Researcher, 33*, 3–13.

Chelimsky, E. (2007). Factors influencing the choice of methods in federal evaluation practice. In G. Julnes & D. Rog (Eds.), *Informing federal policies on evaluation methodology: Building the evidence base for method choice in government sponsored evaluation. New Directions for Evaluation, 113*, 13–33.

Christie, C. A., & Alkin, M. C. (2005). Term. In S. Mathison (Ed.), *Encyclopedia of Evaluation*. Thousand Oaks, CA: Sage.

Datta, L. (1994). Paradigm wars: A basis for peaceful coexistence and beyond. In C. S. Reichardt & S. F. Rallis (Eds.), *The qualitative-quantitative debate: New perspectives. New Directions for Evaluation, 61*, 53–70.

Datta, L. (2007). Looking at the evidence: What variations in practice might indicate. In G. Julnes & D. Rog (Eds.), *Informing federal policies on evaluation methodology: Building the evidence base for method choice in government sponsored evaluation. New Directions for Evaluation, 113*, 35–54.

Derrida, J. (1976). *On grammatology* (G. Spivak, Trans.). Baltimore: Johns Hopkins University Press.

Eisenhart, M., & Towne, L. (2003). Contestation and change in national policy on "scientifically based" education research. *Educational Researcher, 32*, 31–38.

Erickson, F., & Gutierrez, K. (2002). Culture, rigor, and science in educational research. *Educational Researcher, 31*, 21–24.

Feuer, M. J., Towne, L., & Shavelson, R. J. (2002). Scientific culture and educational research. *Educational Researcher, 31*, 4–14.

Glewwe, P., Kremer, M., & Moulin, S. (2001). *Textbooks and test scores: Evidence from a randomized evaluation in Kenya*. Washington, DC: World Bank, Development Research Group.

Glewwe, P., Kremer, M., Moulin, S., & Zitzewitz, E. (2004). Retrospective vs. prospective analyses of school inputs: The case of flip charts in Kenya. *Journal of Development Economics, 74*, 251–268.

Greene, J. C., & Caracelli, V. (1997). Advances in mixed-method evaluation: The challenges and benefits of integrating diverse paradigms. *New Directions for Program Evaluation, 74*.

Greene, J. C., Caracelli, V., & Graham, W. F. (1989). Toward a conceptual framework for multimethod evaluation designs. *Educational Evaluation and Policy Analysis, 11*, 255–274.

Guba, E. G. (1990). The alternative paradigm dialog. In E. G. Guba (Ed.), *The paradigm dialog*. Thousand Oaks, CA: Sage.

House, E. R. (1994). Integrating the quantitative and qualitative. In C. S. Reichardt & S. F. Rallis (Eds.), *The qualitative-quantitative debate: New perspectives. New Directions for Program Evaluation, 61*, 13–22.

Howell, E. M., & Yemane, A. (2006). An assessment of evaluation designs: Case studies of 12 large federal evaluations. *American Journal of Evaluation, 27*, 219–236.

Johnson, R. B., & Onwuegbuzie, A. J. (2004). Mixed methods research: A research paradigm whose time has come. *Educational Researcher, 33*, 14–26.

Joint Committee on Standards for Educational Evaluation. (1994). *The program evaluation standards: How to assess evaluations of educational programs* (2nd ed.). Thousand Oaks, CA: Sage.

Jones, P. W. (1992). *World Bank financing of education: Lending, learning and development*. London: Routledge.

Julnes, G., & Rog, D. (2007a). Current federal policies and controversies over methodology in evaluation. In G. Julnes & D. Rog (Eds.), *Informing federal policies on evaluation methodology: Building the evidence base for method choice in government sponsored evaluation. New Directions for Evaluation, 113*, 1–12.

Julnes, G., & Rog, D. (2007b). Pragmatic support for policies on methodology. In G. Julnes & D. Rog (Eds.), *Informing federal policies on evaluation methodology: Building the evidence base for method choice in government sponsored evaluation. New Directions for Evaluation, 113*, 129–147.

Kovach, H., & Lansman, Y. (2006). World Bank and IMF conditionality: A development injustice. Brussels, Belgium: European Network on Debt and Development (EURODAD) report. Retrieved June 2006, from http://www.globalpolicy.org/socecon/bwi-wto/wbank/index.htm

Lather, P. (1993). Fertile obsession: Validity after poststructuralism. *Sociological Quarterly, 34*, 673–693.

Lincoln, Y. S., & Guba, E. G. (1985). *Naturalistic inquiry*. Thousand Oaks, CA: Sage.

Lipsey, M. (2007). Method choice for government evaluation: The beam in our own eye [commentary]. In G. Julnes & D. Rog (Eds.), *Informing federal policies on evaluation methodology: Building the evidence base for method choice in government sponsored evaluation. New Directions for Evaluation, 113*, 113–115.

Mabry, L. (2002). Postmodern evaluation—or not? *American Journal of Evaluation, 23*, 141–157.

Madaus, G. F., Scriven, M. S., & Stufflebeam, D. L. (Eds.). (1987). *Evaluation models: Viewpoints on educational and human services evaluation*. Boston: Kluwer-Nijhoff.

McGary-Hamilton, E., & Luers, K. W. (2004). *Site visit report for Smaller Learning Communities* [grantee name and grant number suppressed to protect confidentiality]. Portland, OR: Northwest Regional Educational Laboratories.

Mertens, D. (2005). *Research and evaluation in education and psychology: Integrating diversity with quantitative, qualitative, and mixed methods* (2nd ed.). Thousand Oaks, CA: Sage.

Mill, J. S. (1891). *Utilitarianism* (11th ed.). London: Longmans, Green, & Co. (Original work published 1863).

Miller, R. L., & Campbell, R. (2006). Taking stock of empowerment evaluation: An empirical review. *American Journal of Evaluation, 27*, 296–319.

No Child Left Behind Act. (2001). Public Law No. 107–110. 107th Congress, 110 *Congressional Record* 1425, 115 Stat.

Northwest Regional Educational Laboratory (NWREL). (2004). *Smaller Learning Communities site visits: Instructions for project director or coordinator*. Portland, OR: Author.

Pellegrino, J. W., & Goldman, S. R. (2002). Be careful what you wish for—you may get it: Educational research in the spotlight. *Educational Researcher, 31*, 15–17.

Polanyi, M. (1958). *Personal knowledge: Towards a post-critical philosophy*. Chicago: University of Chicago Press.

Psacharopoulos, G., & Woodhall, M. (1991). *Education for development: An analysis of investment choices*. New York: Oxford University Press.

Ravallion, M. (2006). *Evaluating anti-poverty programs* (Policy Research Working Paper 3625). Washington, DC: World Bank.

Rossi, P. H. (1994). The war between the quals and the quants: Is a lasting peace possible? In C. S. Reichardt & S. F. Rallis (Eds.), *The qualitative-quantitative debate: New perspectives. New Directions for Evaluation, 61*, 23–36.

Schemo, D. J. (2004, August 17). Nation's charter schools lagging behind, U.S. test scores reveal. *New York Times*. Retrieved July 21, 2007, from www.nytimes.com/2004/08/17/education/17charter.html

Scriven, M. (1972). Pros and cons about goal-free evaluation. *Evaluation Comment, 3*, 1–3.

Shadish, W. R., & Rindskopf, D. M. (2007). Methods for evidence-based practice: Quantitative synthesis of single-subject designs. In G. Julnes & D. Rog (Eds.), *Informing federal policies on evaluation methodology: Building the evidence base for method choice in government sponsored evaluation. New Directions for Evaluation, 113*, 95–109.

Stufflebeam, D. L. (1994). Empowerment evaluation, objectivist evaluation, and evaluation standards: Where the future of evaluation should not go and where it needs to go. *Evaluation Practice, 15,* 321–338.

Stufflebeam, D. L. (2001). *Evaluation models. New Directions for Evaluation, 89.*

Stufflebeam, D. S., Patton, M. Q., Fetterman, D., Greene, J. G., Scriven, M. S., & Mabry, L. (2001, October). Theories of action in program evaluation. Panel presentation at annual meeting of American Evaluation Association, St. Louis.

U.S. Department of Education (DOE). (2003). Notice of proposed priority: Scientifically based evaluation methods (RIN 1890-ZA00). *Federal Register, 68*(213), 62445–62447.

U.S. Department of Education (DOE). (2005). Scientifically based evaluation methods (RIN 1890-ZA00). *Federal Register, 70*(15), 3586–3589.

U.S. Network for Global Economic Justice. (n.d.). Eliminating IMF and World Bank-promoted user fees for primary health and education. Washington, DC: Author. Retrieved from at http://www.50years.org/action/s26/factsheet3.html

Viadero, D. (2006). Breakaway education research group pulls from diverse disciplines. *Education Week, 26,* 11.

Viadero, D. (2007). AERA stresses value of alternatives to "gold standard." *Education Week, 29,* 12–13.

World Bank (2007). *Impact evaluation.* Retrieved July 10, 2007, from http://web.worldbank.org/WBSITE/EXTERNAL/TOPICS/EXTEDUCATION/0,,contentMDK:20885241~menuPK:2448393~pagePK:210058~piPK:210062~theSitePK:282386,00.html

World Bank Independent Evaluation Group. (2006). *From schooling access to learning outcomes: An unfinished agenda. Evaluation of world bank support to primary education.* Washington, DC: Author. Retrieved July 10, 2007, from http://www.worldbank.org/oed/education

Worthen, B. R., Sanders, J. R., & Fitzpatrick, J. L. (1997). *Program evaluation: Alternative approaches and practical guidelines* (2nd ed.). New York: Longman.

Yin, R. K., & Davis, D. (2007). Adding new dimensions to case study evaluations: The case of evaluating comprehensive reforms. In G. Julnes & D. Rog (Eds.), *Informing federal policies on evaluation methodology: Building the evidence base for method choice in government sponsored evaluation. New Directions for Evaluation, 113,* 75–93.

LINDA MABRY *is a professor of education at Washington State University.*

Nelson, M., & Eddy, R. M. (2008). Evaluative thinking and action in the classroom. In T. Berry & R. M. Eddy (Eds.), *Consequences of No Child Left Behind for educational evaluation. New Directions for Evaluation, 117,* 37–46.

3

Evaluative Thinking and Action in the Classroom

Meta Nelson, Rebecca M. Eddy

Abstract

This case study of one middle school focuses on improving teachers' skills in data-driven decision making through analysis of student work and their own professional practice. The expectation that schools will make adequate yearly progress has pushed evaluation practice down to the teacher level, where teachers are asked to analyze and disaggregate standardized test scores to facilitate instructional decision making that will lead to increased student achievement. The authors analyze this change in relation to No Child Left Behind and to the literature on evaluation capacity building within schools. © Wiley Periodicals, Inc.

Enactment of the No Child Left Behind Act (NCLB, 2001) legislation affects local schools and also has far-reaching implications for the field of evaluation. Schools have been challenged to meet Adequate Yearly Progress (AYP) goals that may or may not be realistic; but to succeed in the current system, educators are required to participate in more extensive evaluative activities than they have in the past. Similarly, the evaluator's role in working with schools has the potential to expand, given the opportunities for helping schools establish and track multiple sources of data, including standardized test data, district- and school-level assessments,

and a multitude of surveys and other evaluative information. Other studies have examined building this type of capacity within schools (Smith & Freeman, 2002; Sutherland, 2004; Trevisan, 2002), but the current case is focused primarily on this process in light of NCLB requirements. Although Scriven (1996) reminds us that the role of a professional evaluator cannot be substituted by those merely participating in evaluative tasks, these tasks are now being performed by educators who often have no formal evaluative training, out of the necessity to achieve success under NCLB. This chapter is a case study of a middle school in California where improving evaluative skills at the school site contributed to improved student achievement.

The Case of Torch Middle School

In 2001, Torch Middle School was ranked among the lowest 20% of middle schools in the state of California. The community surrounding Torch was dominated by a multigenerational gang, whose presence was felt in all aspects of school life from desensitization to violence in the environment to lack of preparation in the home for schooling. The student body was 94% Hispanic, and 80% of the students were identified as educationally disadvantaged. The demographic characteristics of this school community have not changed substantially in the past 5 years. In California, schools are measured on a scale called the Academic Performance Index (API). This is a numeric index ranging from a low of 200 to a high of 1,000; it reflects the performance level of a school on the basis of results of statewide testing. In 2001, Torch was given a score of 435. In 2006, it received an API of 719.

This phenomenal improvement in just 5 years can be matched by only a handful of schools in California. To accomplish this result, the administration and teachers at Torch had to drastically change how they approached the education process. Those changes were made possible by strong administrative leadership and by restructuring many elements of the school day, such as class schedules and teacher assignments. They also included establishment of intense, ongoing professional development focused on student learning and evaluation of student work and teacher practice. Not to be stopped by a lack of funding from the impoverished district, Torch invested in the tedious and time-consuming process of seeking outside funding, which was ultimately furnished by the High Priority Schools Grant Program (California Department of Education, 2007) and the California Community Foundation. While many of the aforementioned changes at Torch most likely contributed to the improvement in student test scores, in this chapter we focus specifically on aspects of these changes that related to evaluation practice.

Principal Leadership. The impetus for change at Torch Middle School was the influence of a new principal with no previous experience as a middle school principal. For the school district, it was a tumultuous period of frequent staff changes and little guidance for teachers and administrators.

NEW DIRECTIONS FOR EVALUATION • DOI: 10.1002/ev

Given these conditions and increasing pressure to meet AYP goals, the principal sought best practices in the literature. He initiated a site-based study of Taking Center Stage (California Department of Education, 2001), the California state document that describes best practices for middle school operation. It was through this study that the school became focused on professional development and data-driven decision making. He mandated that all teachers begin to learn the process and meaning of disaggregated data implied under NCLB. Structural changes were put into place, such as block scheduling, intensive support for second-language learners, comprehensive teacher training, and student regrouping for the differing subject areas. This latter activity placed students in the same performance bands in a subject area (below basic, basic, proficient, and so on) with one teacher for that subject. This produced homogeneous skill levels in each class, which limited the amount of differentiation teachers needed to insert into their lessons. In this way, teachers more appropriately tailored their lessons to meet their students' needs. Also, students who scored far below basic were placed on a list that the assistant principal tracked monthly. Another list of English learners was created for these students to receive special attention and instructional support, including their own summer school session.

In addition to formal staff development by outside experts from the Los Angeles County Office of Education, Springboard Schools, and an external evaluator, the teachers received ongoing support in the form of coaching, modeling, and use of collaborative groups. Staff and administrators relied on a variety of instruments to inform their progress, among them teacher, parent, and student surveys. A new data-management system was put into place to better organize and analyze existing data and new instruments. Torch led the way in mastering its technology and using it to analyze data. All ensuing staff development was provided to support cultivation and honing of the evaluative skills necessary to make good educational decisions. The process of building staff capacity did not originate in response to an external evaluation, but rather from AYP requirements that required improved student achievement each year. However, with the principal's leadership, many of the activities that occurred at Torch mirror sound evaluation practice.

Moving Beyond Adequate Yearly Progress. Torch Middle School, like nearly all schools, is required to demonstrate that students are meeting AYP goals every year. Unfortunately, the data sent back to schools in aggregate form is insufficient as a diagnostic tool. This notion is supported by a plethora of evidence suggesting a single measure of student achievement via high-stakes testing is not conducive to assessing student learning (Amrein & Berliner, 2002). The American Evaluation Association (AEA) issued an official position in objection to such practices (AEA, 2002). Because no single assessment is capable of fostering a complete picture of student learning, the state standardized tests, though mandated by NCLB to measure school and individual success, are insufficient to guide instruction. State tests offer no information about learning patterns for small groups or even individual students. For example, they do not target specific skills such as decoding or figurative language and subsequently yield no information on possible interventions. To find specific student deficit patterns, the state test scores must be disaggregated by unit of content or by specific standard. Although NCLB mandated disaggregation of data by major groups and subgroups, Torch found it necessary to further disaggregate data by grade level, by teacher and individual student, and by individual standard (Black & William, 1998). More specific disaggregated data are necessary to allow teachers to assess individual student performance and design specific interventions for improvement. To continue to meet goals specified under NCLB, we suggest that public school teachers go well beyond the AYP report, use new sets of skills that require evaluating the effectiveness of their current practice, and then make strategic changes to their planning and teaching. Unfortunately, this process can be difficult for even the most experienced educators. Next, we describe specific processes at Torch that allowed teachers to move beyond standardized testing reports to better meet the needs of their students.

Teacher Collaboration and Professional Development. There is an abundance of research that suggests teachers learn necessary skills when they work in collaborative groups (DuFour, DuFour, Eaker, & Karhanek, 2004). When teachers examine student work and plan on the basis of that examination, they maximize their effectiveness as teachers. However, to do this work, they need an array of complex evaluative skills. Specifically, these skills include the ability to access a database to enter or retrieve raw data, create reports such as an item analysis, and align a course-pacing calendar with results from both state and local assessment systems. Only when a collaborative teacher group has mastered these skills can they begin to develop meaningful interventions to improve AYP. At Torch, teachers gradually improved their skills in collaborating around common assessments and analysis of student work. Their discussion of student progress became richer over time with the incorporation of these multiple measures.

Multiple Assessment Systems. In parallel with good evaluation practice, multiple measures of performance are necessary to evaluate students in schools appropriately. To arrive at a reliable analysis of student work, teachers must look at assessment data from a variety of sources for each individual student and, consequently, adapt their teaching to conform to each student's revealed strengths and weaknesses. In addition, they must look at the data for each group of students they teach to determine how they will manage their instructional time with that group. In addition to state sources, the most commonly used data at Torch came from a districtwide local assessment system and from teacher-created assessments. The power to use these data as an evaluative tool was most evident when they were broken down by individual test item. Disaggregated state data were supplied to the teacher by the testing agency, though just to the level of substandard or strand. This allowed the teacher a general idea of the location of strengths and weaknesses; however, to ascertain more relevant information, the specific test items were addressed in the district local assessment system. This system usually relied on multiple choice questions plus adaptations, such as oral responses, diagrams, and essays. The tests were given frequently during the year to show the rate of student progress, as well as at both the beginning and end of the year as diagnostic and summative exams. They were written or edited by district personnel so that they more directly addressed the characteristics of the population in the district.

The final level of evaluative information came from classroom assessments. It is at this level that authentic forms of assessment, such as portfolios, dioramas, and performances, came into play. Mastery of skills that was not apparent in other assessment experiences was often revealed this way. But beyond the type of assessment used at the classroom level, it is the adaptability of the tool to the particular student group that gives it power. A classroom-level assessment can address key concepts according to different degrees of difficulty. The number of questions and the level of difficulty could be adjusted by the teacher to produce maximum information. At Torch, it was a gradual process of allowing teachers to work with and understand multiple assessments to assess the progress of their students appropriately, aided with an electronic data-management system.

Reporting and Data Organization. Most schools and districts are increasingly turning to a computer assessment service or program to organize both their state and local assessment data. This kind of system permits relatively easy access to data for people who need the information but are not professional evaluators. Once the teacher has learned to use this system, reports based on varying forms of disaggregated data are available to teachers to inform planning and instruction. After a teacher has accumulated a collection of disaggregated assessments, he or she can begin to adjust the pacing calendar for the curriculum to be taught in the subject area tested. The areas of weakness for students can be identified and more time allotted for instruction. Conversely, areas of strength can be addressed without giving students unnecessary time to work on mastered skills (McTighe & Wiggins, 1998).

Incorporation of an electronic data-management system at Torch allowed teachers to view and track multiple assessments throughout the year. It was a difficult transition for teachers and administration to view test scores as a public road map that all teachers shared jointly rather than as private information. Groups of teachers worked together to incorporate student scores. As the academic year progressed, teachers used benchmark exams from both the districtwide assessment system and their own classroom-level sources. These tools afforded them feedback on how well the students were progressing toward mastery of the standards being taught. The software also allowed teachers and administrators to create a variety of reports, including item analysis and demographic reports. This created a new level of transparency at which teachers and administrators could easily see individual and aggregate results on state tests for students in their classes. Areas of weakness required adjustments to the pacing calendar in each classroom for reteaching and additional student practice.

The process of learning to use a data-management system was not easy. The software was difficult for novices to use at times, especially because each application had to be learned by each practitioner. There were also technical problems, including data-entry scanners that broke down from the high volume of use. For the first year of use, teachers confined themselves to disaggregating California Standards Test (CST) data on the electronic system; incorporating other data sources was simply overwhelming in this stage. As the years progressed, teachers became more adept at incorporating multiple sources of data in their analysis of students. After a gradual process of familiarizing themselves with the data-management system, teachers eventually created their own classroom-level tests through the software program. This process was filled with trial and error as teachers created and later abandoned common assessments. Throughout the entire process, teachers and administrators became more adept at incorporating other interested individuals in the process.

Involving Multiple Stakeholders. One noteworthy aspect to the processes that occurred at Torch was involvement of multiple stakeholders as a key to changing the environment at the school. Initially, the principal analyzed schoolwide and grade-level patterns of data shared with the school administration and leadership team. Teachers were incorporated into this process gradually, and eventually they performed their own data analyses. As teachers and administrators progressed in their skills, they were able to conduct more sophisticated analyses. Eventually, teachers and administrators became actively involved in showing parents and students what to look for in analyzing the data. It became common practice for all of the information that the teacher collected to be shared with students and their families. For that to happen, students and their parents have an ongoing need for sufficient understanding of assessments as guidance for student achievement. Though it is a difficult process to incorporate an entire community of learners into such thinking (and it is far from a completed process at Torch), it is no longer acceptable for any stakeholder in the school setting to function without these skills.

Evaluation Capacity Building at Torch

Theorists and practitioners have outlined the process of evaluation capacity building (ECB) for those in programs and schools. Stockdill, Baizerman, and Compton (2002) have defined ECB as "the intentional work to continuously create and sustain overall organizational processes that make quality evaluation and its uses routine" (p. 14). King (2002) also highlighted the particular emphasis on ECB in schools and districts and presented a rich example of what ECB looks like in a district in Minnesota. More recent examples can also be found in Huffman, Lawrenz, Thomas, and Clarkson (2006), in which their university partnership was concerned with building evaluation capacity for teachers and graduate students focused on mathematics and science education. These descriptions of ECB have a common element of intentionality to use the process of evaluation to build skills in stakeholders, particularly with the assistance of a professional evaluator. Huffman and colleagues described the "inquiry cycle" used with classroom teachers, which included reviews of national, state, and local district test scores; focusing the evaluation and developing evaluation questions; collecting and analyzing data; developing an action plan; and monitoring results as an ongoing cyclical process. Their description is similar to the process that occurred at Torch Middle School, albeit with a less formal process of the intention to focus all efforts on a formal evaluation process, instead with the stated focus of developing plans for action around test scores and monitoring progress after system changes were instituted.

The process that occurred at Torch Middle School appears to have some of the essential elements of ECB. Although the reform process was guided in part by an external evaluator, most of the activities were generated from staff and administration. This included, but was not limited to, work in collaborative groups, development of assessment systems that more accurately served their needs and their students' needs, and thoughtful reflection and action on how classroom instruction and activities in addition to staff, parent, and teacher survey results related to their students' learning and subsequent improvement on state tests. An analysis of the activities at Torch reflects a current reality that processes similar to ECB are happening and working effectively for schools, although this is not always recognized as such.

In 2005, Torch Middle School teachers were surveyed to ascertain which sources of data were most beneficial to informing their teaching (Mintrop & Trujillo, 2006). The pattern of their responses indicates that they were most comfortable using the data sources they used the longest, particularly relying on state and district assessments. This further suggests that building evaluative capacity in any teaching staff is a long-term process and not all sources of data are valued equally. Additional research in evaluation capacity building may help to illuminate which data are most informative for teachers in improving their skills and subsequent student achievement.

The Disconnect Between Teacher Preparation and School Expectations for Teachers

The ability to analyze and use data to target student achievement in a common effort with other teachers, combined with the ability to teach both students and parents how to look at their own data, has become a prerequisite in a world under NCLB. As if acquisition of this constellation of skills is not sufficiently daunting, NCLB by implication requires that teachers collaborate in planning and analysis groups to ensure consistent instruction from class to class and, therefore, facilitate equal access for all students. This has resulted in unforeseen challenges. Simply put, teachers have not been prepared to do this work.

NCLB's provision for a highly qualified teacher (HQT) in every classroom is based on set qualifications, not on teacher skill. The recent report from the Commission on NCLB (Thompson & Barnes, 2007) highlighted the need for teachers to demonstrate effective practice as opposed to meeting only qualification requirements—essentially a shift from HQTs to highly qualified effective teachers (HQETs). These teachers would be required to demonstrate effectiveness in the classroom through a multiyear process. All teachers, particularly those with few years in the classroom, require training and professional development experiences to develop effective practice. It is our contention that this will happen if novice teachers are able to see lessons modeled by master teachers, receive feedback from experts and peers on their own teaching, and secure training and practice in collaborative data analysis and strategic planning. A recent study of principals (U.S. Department of Education, 2006) indicated that only 41% of professional development emphasized in Title I schools was related to analyzing and interpreting reports of student achievement data; the same percentage was focused on monitoring individual students' progress toward learning goals. In addition, less than one third of professional development focused on differentiated instruction that was based on student assessment data. We believe that teacher training is necessary to demonstrate such skills, but this need is not necessarily being met in the nation's schools or teacher education programs. Few of the teachers currently working in schools today received the necessary training to perform analytical and evaluative activities in their teacher training preparation (Schmoker, 1999). Nor are many school administrators prepared to do this work, or to help their teachers learn these new skills. The basis for the field of evaluation can be predominately seen in the realm of education (Tyler, 1942), but the current system requires that educators in all capacities participate in evaluative activities at the school site much more than they have in the past.

Conclusion

The case of Torch Middle School shows both school districts and local schools a way to take specific steps to build evaluative skills at the site level. Teachers should develop skills in data analysis and collaboration and the ability to align their curricula with common pacing calendars and specific test results. Beyond these general features, the individual schools should be encouraged to develop idiosyncratically in response to their own local nature and needs. One caveat to the success of Torch is the relationship that it had to the district. Given that the district was not able to provide extensive support for the activities at Torch during the time of reform, the school was forced to operate much like an island among other schools. This feature allowed Torch to function relatively free of some of the regulations that accompany most schools expected to function in the context and limitations of a district. We offer this as a particularly noteworthy feature at Torch—that other schools facing similar issues around teacher professional development and school restructuring may have obstacles to overcome other than those in the current case. The success at Torch Middle School cannot be exclusively attributed to increased evaluation capacity. Other factors, such as scheduling changes and consistent discipline policies, may also be responsible for the change in environment. However, what is evident is that teachers' skill at using data to inform instruction to better meet the needs of students was facilitated by good evaluation practice. Although we share Ryan's concern that "the current wave of educational accountability is relegated to an audit function disconnected from improving teaching and learning" (2005, p. 535), Torch was able to address some concerns related to teaching and learning within the current accountability system. In fact, only through a continued, explicit effort at the school site, as well as having the necessary time and money resources, can one expect to see such remarkable change. The unfortunate reality is that this effort is far beyond what one can expect simply from external accountability and disaggregation of data for specific subgroups mandated by NCLB. In the case of Torch Middle School, multiple stakeholders, including administration, teachers, students, and their parents, improved student achievement, and all stakeholders must engage in a cycle of examination of data and adjustment of planning in response to data. In this way, effective interventions can take place on a national scale so that, indeed, no child is left behind.

References

American Evaluation Association. (2002). *American Evaluation Association position statement on high stakes testing in pre-K–12 education.* Retrieved March 1, 2007, from http://www.eval.org/hst3.htm

Amrein, A. L., & Berliner, D. C. (2002). High-stakes testing, uncertainty, and student learning. *Education Policy Analysis Archives, 10*(18). Retrieved June 22, 2007, from http://epaa.asu.edu/epaa/v10n18/

Black, P., & William, D. (1998). *The value of formative assessment.* FairTest Examiner. Cambridge, MA: FairTest.

California Department of Education. (2001). *Taking center stage: A commitment to standards-based education for California's middle grades students.* Sacramento: California Department of Education Press.

California Department of Education. (2007). *HPSGP, II/USP, and CSR resources.* Retrieved July 19, 2007, from http://www.cde.ca.gov/ta/lp/hp/resources.asp

DuFour, R., DuFour, R., Eaker, R., & Karhanek, G. (2004). *Whatever it takes: How professional learning communities respond when kids don't learn.* Bloomington, IN: Solution Tree.

Huffman, D., Lawrenz, F., Thomas, K., & Clarkson, L. (2006). Collaborative evaluation communities in urban schools: A model of evaluation capacity building for STEM education. In D. Huffman & F. Lawrenz (Eds.), *Critical issues in STEM evaluation. New Directions for Evaluation, 109,* 73–85.

King, J. A. (2002). Building the evaluation capacity of a school district. In D. W. Compton, M. Baizerman, & S. H. Stockdill (Eds.), *The art, craft, and science of evaluation capacity building. New Directions for Evaluation, 93,* 63–80.

McTighe, J., & Wiggins, G. (1998). *Understanding by design.* Alexandria, VA: Association for Supervision and Curriculum Development.

Mintrop, H., & Trujillo, T. (2006) *Middle school improvement within the California School Accountability System.* Berkeley, CA: CRESST.

No Child Left Behind Act. (2001). Public Law No. 107–110. 107th Congress, 110 *Congressional Record* 1425, 115 Stat.

Ryan, K. (2005). Making educational accountability more democratic. *American Journal of Evaluation, 26,* 532–543.

Schmoker, M. (1999). *Results: The key to continuous school improvement.* Alexandria, VA: Association for Supervision and Curriculum Development.

Scriven, M. (1996). Types of evaluation and types of evaluator. *American Journal of Evaluation, 17,* 151–161.

Smith, C. L., & Freeman, R. L. (2002). Using continuous system-level assessment to build school capacity. *American Journal of Evaluation, 23,* 307–319.

Stockdill, S. H., Baizerman, M., & Compton, D. W. (2002). Toward a definition of the ECB process: A conversation with the ECB literature. In D. W. Compton, M. Baizerman, & S. H. Stockdill (Eds.), *The art, craft, and science of evaluation capacity building. New Directions for Evaluation, 93,* 7–25.

Sutherland, S. (2004). Creating a culture of data use for continuous improvement: A case study of an Edison Project school. *American Journal of Evaluation, 25,* 277–293.

Thompson, T. G., & Barnes, R. E. (2007). *Beyond NCLB: Fulfilling the promise to our nation's children.* Report of the Commission on No Child Left Behind. Washington, DC: Aspen Institute.

Trevisan, M. S. (2002). Evaluation capacity in K–12 school counseling programs. *American Journal of Evaluation, 23,* 291–305.

Tyler, R. W. (1942). General statement on evaluation. *Journal of Educational Research, 35,* 492–501.

U.S. Department of Education, Office of Planning, Evaluation and Policy Development, Policy and Program Studies. (2006). *Title I accountability and school improvement from 2001 to 2004: Tassie principal survey.* Washington, DC: Author.

META NELSON *is a coordinator of special projects in Bassett Unified School District in southern California and the former assistant principal at Torch Middle School.*

REBECCA M. EDDY *is a research assistant professor in the School of Behavioral and Organizational Sciences at Claremont Graduate University and a former external evaluator at Torch Middle School.*

4

Using Evaluation Data to Strike a Balance Between Stakeholders and Accountability Systems

Lisa N. T. Schmitt, Maria Defino Whitsett

Abstract

A district evaluator in a large Texas district examines new challenges arising since implementation of No Child Left Behind, relating to (1) navigating competing requirements in state and federal accountability systems; (2) evaluating effectiveness of sanctions districts are required to address; (3) using scientifically based research (SBR) to select effective programs and interventions; and (4) initiating SBR given high student mobility, inefficient data-management systems, and competing priorities of local schools. This chapter details these challenges for district-level evaluators and highlights how they can implement processes that strike a balance between supporting decision making and conducting rigorous evaluation. © Wiley Periodicals, Inc.

The Austin Independent School District (AISD) is one of the largest public school districts in Texas, serving approximately 81,000 students on 108 campuses. Like most urban school districts, AISD is ethnically diverse, with students who are mostly identified as Hispanic (55%),

white (28%), and African American (14%). The majority of students in AISD have been deemed economically disadvantaged (60%), and almost one quarter have limited English proficiency (24%). AISD's Department of Program Evaluation maintains a staff of approximately 12 evaluators who work on projects including state and federal grant evaluations, evaluation of district initiatives, districtwide survey research, coordination of external research projects, and ad hoc data requests.

Evaluators in AISD serve multiple functions within the district in addition to their primary role as traditional program evaluators. Not only must they design and implement evaluation projects to monitor various programs throughout the school year, but they must also collect, analyze, interpret, and describe a multitude of additional data for various staff and stakeholders who require timely, accurate information to assist in the district decision-making process. AISD evaluators are instrumental in primary data collection and secondary analyses. Although many programs are not designed specifically to address the accountability goals of No Child Left Behind (NCLB), evaluators frequently summarize accountability data for district staff and incorporate elements of accountability data into their projects because the information is both publicly available and of interest to the district staff and community.

Additionally, district evaluators are often called on to analyze and interpret accountability data for staff and community members thanks to their expertise in quantitative methodology. In the AISD, evaluators must facilitate appropriate use and reporting of both state and federal accountability data. These responsibilities include projecting district and campus accountability ratings prior to official release by the state agency and examining the effects of various sanctions that are applied to campuses not meeting accountability standards. For these reasons, the accountability requirements of NCLB are particularly relevant to the work of district evaluators. Differing, complex state and federal accountability rating systems and sanctions pose a unique challenge for evaluators in Texas.

NCLB also requires that districts select programs that are proven effective through the use of scientifically based research (SBR). District evaluators must employ methods that are deemed appropriate and assist administrators as they review potential district programs. Use and identification of true SBR is sometimes impeded by factors such as time, funding, and available data. Additionally, evaluators frequently are not involved in the initial selection of district programs. The challenges associated with use of accountability data, evaluation of federal sanctions, and SBR are described in the sections that follow.

Accountability Data Required by NCLB

Texas is among the states having an accountability rating system that existed prior to the requirement for a federal accountability system inherent

New Directions for Evaluation • DOI: 10.1002/ev

in NCLB. As recently as 5 years ago, at least 28 states were identified as having tandem or dual state and federal accountability systems (Goertz & Duffy, 2001). Districts in Texas are among those experiencing challenges that are due to the differing state and federal systems for accountability. Both systems embrace similar criteria and data sources, but they differ on features such as the types of assessment included, calculation and definition of indicator measures used to gauge performance on the various assessments, the student groups that are evaluated, and the additional indicators of success that are monitored. For example, among state accountability indicators are performance of African-American, Hispanic, white, economically disadvantaged, and all students on the state's mainstream assessments in reading and English language arts, writing, social studies, mathematics, and science. There is a separate performance indicator for the five student groups on alternative assessments for identified special education participants, pooled across all subject areas. Federal accountability indicators currently are limited to performance only in reading and mathematics but include examination of participation in the assessment programs as well as two additional student groups: those identified as special education and those with limited English proficiency, though the data on regular and alternative assessments (subject to a cap) are pooled together. In addition, the state accountability system requires a satisfactory longitudinal high school completion rate, comprising both the graduation rate and the rate of those continuing in high school, which differs from the graduation rate required to meet Adequate Yearly Progress (AYP) under the federal system. Allowances for growth or improvement are made in both the state and federal systems in Texas, but under NCLB improvement on the state assessment measures is linked to improvement on "other" measures, such as high school graduation rate (or at the elementary and middle school levels, attendance rate).

The assessment framework in Texas also includes additional tests for English language and special education students that are not allowed in the federal system, though they are required components in the state system. This currently results in two dilemmas. First, under the 3% federal cap on alternative off-grade-level testing for special education students, there are students who are treated in federal calculations as "failures" even though they were tested appropriately according to state guidelines and even though those individuals actually met the state's standards. Second, identified students who are required to take the off-grade-level assessment in the 2006–2007 school year will be treated as nonparticipants in AYP calculations unless those students have also taken field tests in a new program designed to replace the current one by next year. In other words, required tests in one system that impose high stakes for the individual students are considered invalid in the other system. In a recent example, one high school in AISD with a reputation for excellence initially was deemed "academically unacceptable" by the state system because of special education students' low passing rate on the state's alternative assessments; yet the same school made AYP in that year because the high performance rate of the other students could absorb the impact of special education students' performance on the alternative tests in the pooled calculation of AYP.

The federal system's requirement that improvement on test participation or passing rates be tied to improvement on the "other" measure creates interesting classification scenarios, as well; for instance, an elementary school demonstrated tremendous improvement on test-passing rate, but because the attendance rate for that same student group did not also increase, the school was determined to have not met AYP for the year. The school's attendance rate routinely is extremely high (approaching 98%), and it dropped slightly from the year before by mere tenths of a percentage point. Unfortunately, instead of being recognized for vast academic improvement with relatively strong attendance, the school was dubbed a failure under NCLB. Evaluators must regularly include descriptions that capture these complexities in reporting accountability results for various purposes.

These dual accountability systems require evaluators to develop core indicators that respond to both systems and draw data from multiple sources to triangulate student progress. As has been noted, districts and schools in Texas have sometimes received state and federal accountability ratings that seem contradictory. State agency data indicate that 144 Texas campuses meeting AYP in 2006 were rated academically unacceptable in the state accountability system, and 296 campuses that were rated academically acceptable in 2006 under the state accountability system failed to make AYP that same year (Texas Education Agency, 2007). This represents an incongruence of state and federal ratings for more than 5% of campuses in Texas. These inconsistencies are caused by differing requirements and limitations of the two rating systems. For example, a school may be rated as acceptable or better using state criteria but may also fail to make AYP in not meeting certain federal criteria, such as the 95% participation rate or the required passing percentage for students with limited English proficiency. Discrepancies such as these pose challenges for evaluators, who must make interpretations to understand the progress that students, schools, and the district are making toward meeting requirements of NCLB, and who also must accomplish the difficult task of relaying results to district stakeholders who may not understand the intricacies of each system.

In addition to these inconsistencies in rating systems, in Texas there have been specific challenges related to implementation of the state assessment program. For example, complications arose when the state transitioned from the Texas Assessment of Academic Skills (TAAS) to the Texas Assessment of Knowledge and Skills (TAKS), primarily because of a lack of comparable data. During the transition period, it was not possible to measure student progress or improvement over time with any accuracy. Test-passing standards for the new TAKS have been phased in over time, as have the passing percentages required to obtain specific ratings under each system. Because of the transition from TAAS to TAKS, baseline data for AYP are not available prior to 2003, and measures of progress have been difficult to calculate. For this reason, evaluators have faced challenges interpreting and describing longitudinal data to district stakeholders.

Evaluation of Sanctions Required by NCLB

When schools fail to meet standards, districts are required to implement a series of mandatory sanctions from NCLB. The two most notable early sanctions are School Choice and use of Supplemental Service Providers (SSPs) for Supplemental Educational Services (SESs). A Title I school that has not made AYP for 2 consecutive years must offer students the choice to transfer to another public school within the district. If the school does not make AYP for a third consecutive year, students from low-income families are eligible to receive SES, such as tutoring and remedial classes from a state-approved SSP. Several issues complicate evaluating the effectiveness of these sanctions. First, there is a mismatch between the legislation, which allows SSPs to serve any low-income student in a school that fails to make AYP, and the "intent" of the legislation, which is to address the academic needs of those students with deficiencies in mathematics and reading. This mismatch makes interventions less targeted and renders desired outcomes less likely to be identified—even when they occur for some individuals. A recent case in point involves a parental request for tutoring in AP chemistry by an SSP. The National Education Association (NEA) recommends targeting School Choice and SESs, to the specific subgroups that fail to meet AYP (NEA, 2006). This would create interventions that are more congruent with the goals of NCLB and would also allow evaluators to examine the effectiveness of interventions with more precision. However, to date this recommendation has not yet been implemented.

There is also a mismatch between the philosophy of school choice and the tendency for stakeholders to desire information about potentially adverse academic effects of school choice on the receiving school. School choice is intended to foster an opportunity for students in low-performing schools to experience an education at a school that is not low performing. However, district staff and community members may desire information about the test-passing percentage before and after students transfer from a low-performing school to the receiving school. Evaluators must balance the legislative requirement with research questions that are appropriate, such as monitoring progress for those students who choose to exercise the option to transfer.

In addition to the complications of evaluating the effectiveness of each sanction on its own, the challenge is compounded when schools receive more than one of these sanctions. Students in some schools may choose to exercise the school choice transfer option, receive SES, transfer and also receive SES, or do none of these. The various combinations of these options cause difficulty for evaluators, particularly when students move in and out of categories throughout the school year.

Precision in evaluation of school choice and SES also proves difficult in districts such as Austin, where students frequently move from school to school or in and out of the district. A highly mobile student population makes tracking student-level data difficult. The variety of service providers also makes evaluation of effectiveness difficult, particularly when service providers do not track student participation. The lack of commonly maintained data among providers causes inconsistencies in the quality of evaluation that is possible for these programs. For example, evaluators would want to consider students' attendance at tutoring sessions in attempting to determine the effectiveness of these interventions; however, these data are rarely available. To obtain the necessary data for meaningful evaluation, district evaluators may be required to work with a variety of agencies and other district staff to implement and monitor new information collection systems that can accommodate the complex data necessary to follow students in and out of schools and programs throughout the school year and beyond. Evaluators must plan ahead to ensure that student information systems are capable of housing the data necessary to inform research in these areas, especially in light of complex issues such as student mobility and extent of exposure to, or participation in, the tutoring services.

Qualitative data collection may also be needed to understand impediments to full implementation of SES; for instance, the legal requirement is that SES occur outside the regular school day and SES can only be provided after parental signatures are obtained on an individual student plan. These are both major impediments to participation in SES for urban district students. Monitoring participation rate alone would never clarify the nature of these implementation issues for students.

As sanctions become more severe and likely more widespread over time, evaluators and accountability staff must expend ever more energy monitoring or anticipating student performance in areas that will be used to assess AYP. Schools as well as districts are required to make AYP. To prepare for sanctions and other changes if schools do not make AYP, evaluation information is often required before the final accountability ratings are released. Official state and federal ratings in Texas are not released until the summer prior to the start of the school year, which does not allow districts sufficient time for such broad-scale efforts as school leadership changes or designation of schools that will receive transfer students. Evaluators must supply accurate, timely information concerning student performance so that appropriate planning can take place before the start of the next school year.

In Texas, these considerations include whether a school is expected to meet both federal and state accountability standards. This type of information is necessary well before the school year begins because of implications for district operations, such as adequate opportunity for parental notifications, bus routes, school capacity, and program planning. Additionally, given the differing state and federal rating systems, it is critical that evaluators closely monitor data collection to "predict" performance in both systems to identify schools that are eligible to receive students under both systems. This becomes particularly challenging in Texas, where state legislation requires school reconstitution after designation as year 2 academically unacceptable status on the basis of state criteria, while federal legislation requires reconstitution after year 5 school improvement status. In addition, districts must prepare for the increasingly likely event that no school at a given level (for example, high schools) within the district will meet both state and federal standards. In this case, evaluators may be called on to examine all aspects of school data in ways that have not been previously explored, to give district administrators information necessary to make difficult and politically charged decisions concerning the future of certain schools and principals.

Scientifically Based Research at the District

According to the U.S. Department of Education, NCLB "sets forth rigorous requirements to ensure that research is scientifically-based" (U.S. Department of Education, 2007). SBR is described as research that involves using an experimental and control group design, and randomized trials are considered the "gold standard" for SBR (Reyna, 2002). Implementing SBR at the district level is complicated by conducting the types of research studies that qualify as scientifically based and having the staff with the requisite skills in experimental design and analysis.

Research Methods. District evaluators must grapple with two primary issues related to SBR at the district level. First, even though NCLB calls for using programs proven effective through randomized trials and experimental and control group designs, district practices frequently do not lend themselves to such research. Conducting experimental studies is difficult when a targeted intervention is desired. Second, student and teacher mobility frequently result in attrition from programs, thus compromising the size and generalizability of observations and results for remaining groups of participants.

Schools and districts take great care to tailor programs and interventions to the needs of specific student groups. Students are selected for various services according to their assessed level of need; thus, random assignment to treatment conditions is both unlikely and undesirable. To assign students randomly to experimental and control groups would potentially exclude the neediest students from receiving the necessary intervention. Denying students the opportunity for intervention may be considered a violation of the "do no harm" principle, a primary ethical responsibility for evaluators.

Evaluators may use regression discontinuity to allow assignment of students to intervention programs on the basis of need. However, this technique requires larger sample sizes to obtain the same statistical rigor as randomized group assignment, which can be challenging even in a large district because funding and unique target populations may limit the size of intervention groups. In addition, neither randomized group assignment nor regression discontinuity can eliminate the "cross-contamination" that may occur when other teachers or school staff adopt the promising practices of the intervention group. Cross-contamination also occurs naturally in large urban districts, such as Austin, because of high student and teacher mobility.

For these reasons, evaluators must learn and employ a variety of strategies that include both experimental and quasi-experimental research methods. They also must understand and use sophisticated analytical techniques, such as multilevel modeling (for instance, hierarchical linear modeling or HLM), that can remove variance in outcomes that are due to preexisting group differences. Statistical techniques, such as HLM and other advanced statistical methods, have become critical to the ability of district evaluators to conduct research that may be accepted as scientifically based in the absence of randomized control group experimental design. Evaluators are challenged to learn and implement these design and analysis strategies, spending both time and money toward that end.

Staffing Issues. One of the challenges presented to district evaluators by NCLB's requirement for SBR is that other district staff may not have the background necessary to distinguish programs that are truly based on scientific research. Although many programs and interventions claim to be research-based, further examination often reveals otherwise. Staff who are responsible for selecting or designing programs do not always know the difference between existing programs that are supported by rigorous research and those that are not. Sometimes those that claim to be research-based are misleading. For example, evaluators in Austin discovered that a program marketed as "research-based" was merely developed from a literature review of research in the general topic area, but no scientific research was conducted to demonstrate the effectiveness of the program itself. This discovery was the result of an evaluator's desire to review the SBR concerning the program. Only after conversation with the program developer was the lack of SBR revealed. Evaluators are among the limited number of district staff who are likely to recognize a claim of SBR that is unfounded. As a result, district evaluators may be asked to respond by conducting internal experimental studies so that district administrators can be more informed about the effectiveness of certain programs. However, conducting SBR within the district is difficult, for a number of reasons, some of which follow.

Use of programs that are based on SBR requires that districts attract and retain staff capable of conducting and understanding scientific studies. Large districts such as Austin continue to seek job candidates who are skilled in techniques such as HLM and other advanced statistical techniques. However, recent graduates trained in these relatively new methods often have little real-world educational experience. Districts are challenged to find candidates with both the necessary skill set for conducting SBR and the experience to enter public education without a need for extensive on-the-job training. Alternatively, existing staff must be trained in the latest statistical method-ologies, which can be time-consuming and expensive, a major challenge to public institutions with limited budgets and staff who are already assigned to multiple ongoing projects. Additionally, new techniques and research methodologies may frustrate those seasoned evaluators who have employed other strategies effectively for many years. Frustration among all district evaluators may be compounded by the discrepancy between the types of data that must be collected and submitted to the state agency to fulfill federal grant-reporting requirements and the type of data that should be used (1) by the federal government to conduct SBR as outlined in NCLB and (2) by dis-trict evaluators for determining program effectiveness.

Staff retention can be problematic for districts in this context where funding for experimental evaluation has been reduced. For example, the majority of all school districts received less Title I money in 2005–2006 than the previous school year, and overall Title I funding was reduced even fur-ther in 2006–2007 (National Education Association, 2006). In addition, up to 20% of districts' Title I money must be set aside to pay for sanctions such as SES and transportation for School Choice. These funding issues carry implications for evaluators.

District evaluators are faced with the contradictory experience of being required to learn methods appropriate for SBR when time often does not allow them to use such skills. A potential side effect of this circumstance is that evaluators may become discouraged with the lack of time, money, or expertise available for conducting SBR. Evaluators who are qualified to do such research may seek employment in another environment where their competencies are fully used.

Resources for Conducting SBR. Although NCLB does not require dis-trict staff specifically to conduct SBR, legislation requires consideration of programs that are based on rigorous research. Because many district initia-tives are locally developed, districts are responsible for ensuring that such programs are proven effective with methods considered appropriate for SBR. However, both the funding and time necessary to conduct such research are scarce, and staff are consumed with efforts to collect the basic information required for federal grant reports, which often does not include the data that would be necessary for conducting experimental or quasiexperimental studies of program effectiveness.

In many districts such as Austin, evaluators are funded from one or more specific grant budgets to work on evaluation activities related to those grants. If overall funding for a particular grant is reduced, evaluators may receive a smaller portion than before to allow programmatic expenditures to remain steady. This can cause a reduction in the number of evaluators supported by the district and cause evaluators to seek additional grants to maintain full-time employment status. Staff may be required to evaluate more programs on the basis of multiple funding allocations. As a result, evaluators are left with only the resources to perform basic tasks such as tracking participants, documenting expenditures, and reporting general outcomes for each program as required by grants. These reporting mandates frequently do not include information necessary for true program evaluation, so district staff must find creative ways to collect, analyze, and interpret meaningful program data while also completing federal grant reports.

Data Challenges. Even if evaluators are able to employ the sophisticated methods required for SBR, other challenges exist. Lack of sufficient sample sizes and lack of generalizability may impede progress in this area. District evaluators often cannot control either the number of program participants or the specific program parameters. Interventions sometimes are designed for use with a small group of students or teachers with unique needs, and group size may be limited to as few as one classroom of students or only a small sample of teachers. Small sample sizes are not appropriate for many statistical techniques, including those that are considered to be scientifically based. In addition to small sample sizes failing to produce the statistical power necessary for certain methods, unique participant characteristics may restrict the ability to generalize findings to other settings. These contextual limitations can hinder implementation of SBR even when time and resources are available to conduct such studies.

Conclusion

The accountability standards and sanctions that are required by NCLB have expanded the work of evaluators in AISD beyond traditional program evaluation to include such duties as analyzing and describing accountability data for decision makers and stakeholders, evaluating the effects of sanctions, and offering assistance related to SBR. These tasks must be completed despite a decrease in federal funding for evaluation while federal grant-reporting requirements persist.

Districts such as AISD must actively seek evaluators who can understand and employ methodology deemed appropriate for SBR as described in NCLB, and they must also work to maximize the efficiency of data collection across programs and purposes. Both are necessary to conduct meaningful program evaluation while also collecting the data necessary for grant reporting and for making accountability-related decisions. To facilitate these activities, evaluators must strive to streamline data-collection efforts so that staff are able to share information for multiple purposes and conduct comprehensive program evaluations in the face of competing requirements. To maximize efficiency, they also must collaborate with district-management information staff to develop automated data collection and reporting systems, where possible, and take an integrated approach to the planning process for the various program evaluations that are conducted within the district each year. It is also critical for evaluators to establish clear communication with program managers and district leadership to ensure that selected programs are based on true SBR. When rigorous research methods are needed to establish program effectiveness, evaluators may be required to work with other district staff to obtain the funding necessary to support such studies.

Evaluators in AISD participate in ongoing professional development activities to enhance their understanding of evaluation methodology, learn how best to use technology, improve management strategies, and understand legislative requirements. Staff are also challenged to design and implement at least one "special project" in addition to collecting and analyzing data necessary for federally mandated reporting. Inclusion of these research projects helps to ensure that high-quality program evaluations are conducted in the context of limited resources and promotes a stimulating environment for staff who enjoy employing rigorous research methodology. What is most exciting under NCLB is the possibility of pursuing some conceptually elegant research and evaluation work in the realm of "aptitude-treatment interactions." That is, evaluators have some opportunity to use fairly sophisticated methods to examine *which* students' needs are best met under which set(s) of interventions, leading to the best educational outcomes.

NCLB presents evaluators with multiple opportunities for SBR in areas of critical importance, such as the effects of school choice and supplemental services, and participation in developing technically rigorous growth models to more fully capture district or school effectiveness. However, evaluators must also prepare a variety of additional information that is crucial to district decision makers as they struggle with the complexities of implementing the law. Striking a balance between these two functions becomes perhaps one of the greatest challenges of all, because district leadership legitimately needs both forms of information to effectively manage limited resources relative to programs identified as being effective. Through use of automated data-collection systems, an integrated approach to evaluation activities, ongoing professional development, a keen eye for opportunities to engage in research and development work related to the goals of NCLB, and clear communication with district leadership, evaluators in AISD are able to meet the new demands of NCLB while continuing to serve their role as traditional program evaluators.

References

Goertz, M. E., & Duffy, M. (2001). *Assessment and accountability systems in the 50 states: 1999–2000* (Research Rep. No. RR-046). University of Pennsylvania, Consortium for Policy Research in Education.

NEW DIRECTIONS FOR EVALUATION • DOI: 10.1002/ev

National Education Association. (2006, July). *ESEA: It's time for a change! NEA's positive agenda for the ESEA reauthorization.* Retrieved May 8, 2007, from http://www.nea.org/lac/esea/images/posagenda.pdf

No Child Left Behind Act. (2001). Public Law No. 107–110. 107th Congress, 110 *Congressional Record* 1425, 115 Stat.

Reyna, V. (2002, February). *What is scientifically based evidence? What is its logic?* Use of Scientifically Based Research in Education Working Group Conference, Washington, DC. Retrieved May 8, 2007, from http://www.ed.gov/nclb/methods/whatworks/research/page_pg3.html

Texas Education Agency. (2007, March). Data provided at Commissioner's Accountability Advisory Committee meeting, Austin.

U.S. Department of Education. (2007). *Questions and answers on No Child Left Behind: Doing what works.* Retrieved May 8, 2007, from http://www.ed.gov/nclb/methods/whatworks/doing.html#2

LISA N. T. SCHMITT is an evaluation supervisor in the Department of Program Evaluation at Austin Independent School District, Texas.

MARIA DEFINO WHITSETT is the executive director of accountability for the Austin Independent School District.

NEW DIRECTIONS FOR EVALUATION • DOI: 10.1002/ev

Guillén-Woods, B. F., Kaiser, M. A., & Harrington, M. J. (2008). Responding to account-
ability requirements while promoting program improvement. In T. Berry & R. M. Eddy
(Eds.), *Consequences of No Child Left Behind for educational evaluation. New Directions for
Evaluation, 117,* 59–70.

5

Responding to Accountability Requirements While Promoting Program Improvement

*Blanca Flor Guillén-Woods, Monica A. Kaiser,
Maura J. Harrington*

Abstract

*The impact of No Child Left Behind (NCLB) is usually understood in relation
to schools and districts, but the legislation has also affected community-based
organizations that operate school-linked programs. This case study of an after-
school program in California demonstrates how educational accountability systems that emphasize students' academic achievement and scientifically based
research prompted evaluators to modify evaluation questions, methods, and analytic techniques. The external demands of NCLB transformed the evaluation to
support the relevance and value of this community-based program within the
evolving framework of accountability for the school.* © Wiley Periodicals, Inc.

Recent emphasis on the No Child Left Behind legislation (NCLB, 2001)
and its research guidelines for evaluation has resulted in increased outcome evaluation activities in K–12 settings. Under NCLB, schools have
been held accountable for student academic achievement through use of standardized test scores. Though these accountability efforts have not always

shown a strong relationship with school improvement (Nichols, Glass, & Berliner, 2005), they have succeeded in creating a school environment that is increasingly focused on high-stakes testing. In this environment, even community-based organizations with school-linked programs, not directly under NCLB, feel the pressure to demonstrate explicitly their contribution to improved student academic performance. Over the last 5 years, this increased focus on measuring academic progress through standardized tests has had positive and negative impacts on local educational agencies (LEAs) and community-based organizations (CBOs) and their local evaluators.

This chapter explores this impact through a case study of a program in Los Angeles to illustrate how evaluation decisions have been indirectly affected by NCLB and, more specifically, scientifically based research (SBR). The case study presented here is of Woodcraft Rangers (WR), a community-based organization providing after-school services at school sites in southern California.

Brief Overview of Woodcraft Rangers

The primary goal of the Woodcraft Rangers after-school program is to extend schools' capacities to provide a safe, supportive environment beyond the school day and help students improve social, behavioral, and learning skills that contribute to improved school achievement. The Woodcraft program model draws on best practices in the after-school field and on research-based practices identified by organizations such as the National Youth Development Center, Clark and Associates, Public/Private Ventures, the Harvard Family Research Project, and others. Woodcraft Rangers has offered after-school programs in more than 40 schools in Los Angeles County through funding from the California Department of Education's (CDE) After School Education and Safety Program (ASES), U.S. Department of Education's 21st Century Community Learning Center Grants, and Los Angeles City funds. To meet the program's evaluation needs, including their funding agencies' requirements, Lodestar Management/Research was contracted in 1997 and continues to work on the program's current evaluations.

Woodcraft Rangers Case Study

This case study focuses on how WR and its evaluator-modified evaluation activities to measure the program's progress toward program improvement and meet the reporting requirements of the funders. Further, the case study describes how evaluation decisions and approaches were indirectly affected by the NCLB legislation. Although this case study illustrates only specific changes in the evaluation activities of one school-linked program, the evaluators observed similar changes in several school-linked programs.

General Evaluation Approach. During the late 1990s, Woodcraft was in its early stages of evaluation—collecting information on the number of students who attended the program, their demographics, retention rate and program satisfaction level. By 2001, even prior to the signing of NCLB, the program's leadership was aware of the shifting school environment and began feeling pressure from partner schools for increased evaluation efforts focused on academic outcome data for participants. It was at this point that WR began working most intensively with its evaluators. The first step in designing the evaluation was identifying the research questions. WR had several program goals and key stakeholders. Similar to other programs, WR also had limited funds for evaluation, making it a challenge to answer all of their research questions each year. Thus, the core evaluation questions had to be identified. One of the key questions asked during this phase was, "Does the value of the information outweigh the effort to obtain it?" In the era of NCLB, the answer to this question was a resounding yes when measures of academic performance were included.

The evaluator worked collaboratively with WR to create an evaluation plan that incorporated core research questions related to academic achievement, youth development, and program improvement (see Table 5.1). Note

Table 5.1. Evaluation Questions Before and After No Child Left Behind

Initial Evaluation Questions	Evaluation Questions Refined Over the Years for Program Improvement
Are youths and parents satisfied with the program? Did we reach our objectives to: – Increase social and communication skills? – Develop youths' acquisition of new skills and knowledge? – Increase self-confidence?	1. What population is WR serving? 2. To what extent does WR increase youth engagement in after-school activities? 3. Do WR programs help schools keep students safely occupied during after-school hours? 4. To what extent are school administrators, parents, and participating students satisfied with the program quality? 5. Do students who participate in WR attend school more regularly? 6. To what extent do students who attend WR develop prosocial interests and behaviors and avoid at-risk behaviors? *Enhancements to the Evaluation Influenced by NCLB* 7. To what extent do WR participants improve their attitude toward school and learning? 8. To what extent do WR participants improve their learning skills and habits? 9. Is participation in WR associated with a higher level of academic achievement?

NEW DIRECTIONS FOR EVALUATION • DOI: 10.1002/ev

that only three questions are directly related to academic performance (Questions 7 to 9); the others are more closely related to the outcome areas WR directly addresses or to their process evaluation questions.

Although NCLB facilitated the program's decision to include standardized test scores, SBR guidelines indicated that the gold standard for evaluation was in using experimental methods, especially random assignment (DOE, 2003). Though not the only option, preference for this approach was clearly recognized by the schools, the community-based organizations providing services to the schools, and, of course, their evaluators. All three entities realized that even if not required, they should employ this methodology whenever possible to be competitive for funds and demonstrate their effectiveness.

WR was no exception, as the program decided to include a comparison group design to address some of their research questions. Despite the emphasis on random assignment, WR would not deny program access for the purposes of evaluation. To navigate the challenge of creating a comparison group, the evaluators decided to use a post-hoc comparison group at the end of each program year by means of district databases. Agreements with the district for data sharing on participants extended to data sharing on all students in a Woodcraft school. In fact, one of the unexpected benefits of NCLB was the opportunity for community-based programs and districts to collaborate more closely in accessing academic data electronically. That is, as NCLB mandated that school districts improve their systems for tracking student achievement, much more data became accessible to CBOs with school-linked programs. Using these data, analyses comparing participants to nonparticipants (statistically controlling for demographic and baseline measures) became the centerpiece of the WR evaluation following NCLB. Over the years, these analyses positively affected the program because WR was able to demonstrate that it had a legitimate, important role on school campuses. The academic findings were particularly useful because they were presented along with results from the paired sample t-tests examining changes on participants' social skills, at-risk behavior, and attitude toward school.

The local evaluator and WR collaborated to conduct this type of evaluation for several years while, at the same time, addressing the challenge of including process and other outcome measures with essentially the same evaluation budget. Although academic measures were furnished electronically by the school district for participating schools, these data still had to be merged across years and matched with WR records for participating students. Completing this process for more than 30 schools, as well as recoding data, computing changes, and selecting comparison groups, was extremely time-intensive. Although the program wanted to continue including a comparison group design given the weight it held for WR stakeholders, the cumulative evidence from these analyses suggested that compared to nonparticipants, participants made significant academic gains only after they were in the program for 6 months or more (Lodestar, 2005). Thus, the program was interested in finding ways of attracting more students and retaining them for 6 months or more. WR became interested in additional process-related questions: (1) What attracts students to WR? (2) What individual-level characteristics are related to how long students attend WR? and (3) What program-level characteristics are related to how long students attend WR? Because WR's evaluation budget was limited, it was not possible to conduct the full-impact evaluation while conducting an in-depth process evaluation. The solution reached was to focus on the impact evaluation one year and then focus on the process evaluation questions in other years. See Table 5.2 for a recap of the enhancements made to the evaluation approach.

Data Collection, Instruments, and Systems. Whereas WR presumed that positive social-emotional changes for youths would affect their academic performance, measuring the indirect impact on academics was not the primary focus of their program. However, under NCLB, this perspective had to change. The challenge for the local evaluator was to create a feasible data-collection plan that incorporated these additional measures while not over-burdening the Woodcraft staff, school principals, teachers, or students. Methodologies used included participant satisfaction reports, youth surveys, parent interviews, and an outcome report for each participant completed by WR staff. WR's local evaluator believed that use of multiple methods, sources, and time points for triangulation of findings (Greene, Caracelli, & Graham, 1989) was both sensible and appropriate. The next section summarizes each of these methods and examines how each was revised to respond to the increasing emphasis on academic achievement outcomes.

Participation Records. Demographic (gender, ethnicity, age), school (current school and grade level), and program attendance data were

Table 5.2. Evaluation Approach Before and After No Child Left Behind

Initial Evaluation Approach	Adjustments Made to Evaluation Approach Influenced by NCLB
Focus placed on socioemotional outcomes while attempts were made to examine some academic outcomes	Increasingly focused on measuring academic outcomes, specifically standardized test scores, while maintaining some socioemotional measures
Paired sample t-tests conducted to measure changes for participants in socioemotional and academic outcomes	Added quasi-experimental design with comparison group regression analyses to assess the impact of the program on academic outcomes
Emphasis on evaluation for program improvement and meeting basic funder reporting requirements	Emphasis on impact evaluation while rotating inclusion of some process questions in different years

collected by program staff and stored in the Woodcraft Rangers tracking database. Even though Woodcraft had always collected this information, it was previously stored in Excel spreadsheets (or on hard copy) and children were not tracked by a unique identifier. With NCLB pressure to examine individual-level growth across time, the local evaluator adjusted the tracking system to address these emerging evaluation needs. Adjustments were made so that each student who attended the program obtained a primary key that uniquely identified him or her. This identifier also linked demographic information with student program attendance and responses on the Woodcraft-specific instruments (that is, youth surveys). In addition, Woodcraft staff were trained on how to collect the participants' unique school identifier, required to link them to their district data records.

Academic Records. WR experienced some benefits from NCLB related to accessing school data (discussed earlier), but there were other challenges in using standardized test scores as a measure of program outcomes. The primary challenge was changes in the tests used by the state. From 1998 to 2002, a norm-referenced test (the Stanford 9) was used in California, allowing local evaluators to conduct longitudinal analyses of individual student improvement. However, in 2003, this test was replaced by another norm-referenced test (the California Achievement Test 6th edition, or CAT6). These tests assessed how well each student was achieving academically compared to a national sample of students tested in the same grade at the same time of the school year. One year later, the state made another change and no longer required that the CAT6 be administered to all grade levels. Thus, the evaluation had to rely on one criterion-referenced test: the California Standardized Test (CST). The changes in tests made it impossible to use standardized test scores in longitudinal analyses (one of the goals under NCLB), given that individual student scores could not be compared across years.

The CST scores presented another challenge. The CST test was designed to be grade- and subject-specific to determine student proficiency levels: far below basic, below basic, basic, proficient, and advanced. This test was designed for cohort analyses, not for individual-level student tracking; therefore, it was considered inappropriate for longitudinal analyses of student progress. Evaluators are currently collaborating with other local evaluators and district evaluators to identify how best to use this test for purposes of evaluating an after-school program.

Participant Surveys. Participant surveys were designed prior to NCLB to measure aspects of youth development, the primary focus of WR. The evaluators, in collaboration with program staff, designed a two-page survey to be completed by students when they first joined the Woodcraft program and again at the end of each academic school year. The surveys assessed constructs related to school attitude, academic skills, personal sense of efficacy, problem-solving skills, and risk-taking behaviors. WR and their evaluators made it a priority to keep the participant surveys in the evaluation plan even with the increased academic focus. Accepting the reality that many stakeholders wanted to know if the program contributed to improved test scores, WR did not want to exclude how youth-development results directly related to their activities. This was particularly important considering the difficulty of an after-school program to demonstrate a significant impact on test scores, when the evidence suggests that schools with 6 hours per day of instruction found it difficult to increase test scores substantially (Kane, 2004). However, recently WR included additional youth-development skills that could lead to academic improvement, such as leadership, study skills, and exposure to new activities.

The Woodcraft participant survey used a pre-post methodology, though it was not the most cost-effective approach given the staff time needed for administering it twice a year. Another approach often used to measure change is a retrospective measure, which would allow participants to report the extent to which the program made an impact. Retrospective change tools would require one instead of two administration points, and some researchers have found them to be more valid in measuring awareness, knowledge, and attitudes than pre-post measures (Pratt, McGuigan, & Katzev, 2005). To explore the validity of using this methodology with WR, during one year, the post student survey was revised to include a few retrospective items that reflected the same concepts as several of the items included in the pre-post measures. The findings from the retrospective change measures and the changes calculated from the pre-post measures were highly correlated. The retrospective change items were also strongly correlated with staff assessments (recently taken out of the evaluation). However, for this methodology to meet the scientific standards of rigor under NCLB and SBR, the surveys would have needed to include a control group and random assignment, which was not possible for WR given resources and program design. Although the pre-post design completed by program participants does not meet these standards, the program and local evaluator found that some funders still preferred the pre-post design.

Focus Groups and School Staff Interviews. Both prior to and after NCLB, qualitative data were collected from parents and school administrators through interviews and focus groups. These collection efforts were designed primarily for internal purposes of process evaluation, which was encouraged for program improvement (Gomby & Larson, 1992). They were conducted at the end of the program year with parents of participants and with school principals, soliciting their perception of program benefits and their satisfaction with the program. This was helpful for program improvement because it identified potential concerns and helped strengthen ties with the school sites. Given limited funds for evaluation, Woodcraft staff conducted the staff interviews and parent focus groups rather than the evaluation staff. Woodcraft primarily reserved the external evaluation budget for test-score analysis and comparison-group activities. The evaluator did, however, design the instruments and protocols, trained Woodcraft administrative staff on how to conduct them, and incorporated the findings into the final report. This permitted collection of process data within the larger outcome evaluation. Although the quality of the data may have been affected given that program staff conducted the focus groups, this was one of the compromises required to create an evaluation that was responsive to the program's information needs within an NCLB framework.

During a year where there was a process evaluation focus, the evaluators were able to conduct a series of focus groups with students. The focus groups were conducted to obtain rich feedback about successful and unsuccessful recruitment and retention strategies. Half of the focus groups were conducted with students with less than 3 months of participation, while the other half was students who been in the program for more than 6 months. The sessions yielded rich contextual information that WR used for program improvement. The evaluators were able to conduct these sessions because comparison-group analyses on academic performance were not carried out that year. Unfortunately, limited evaluation funds could not accommodate both. The adjustments made to the data collection efforts and instruments are summarized in Table 5.3.

The Value of Evaluation at All Levels. Woodcraft leadership realized very early in the program's development that strong evaluation was necessary for growth and improvement. A key challenge after NCLB was to meet all of the internal and increased external expectations while still operating on a limited evaluation budget. WR realized the only way to accomplish this was for program staff to be actively involved in evaluation activities. Evaluation was integrated into the organization in a number of ways: (1) the

Table 5.3. Data Collection, Instruments, and Systems

Initial Data Collection, Instruments, and Systems	Adjustments Made to Data Collection, Instruments, and Systems Influenced by NCLB
Primary data-collection activities were implemented to document participant attendance and demographic information	Data collection systems became more sophisticated, enabling evaluators to merge data from different sources, including district files; increased attempts to examine longitudinal impacts
Participant survey designed to be cost-effective and focused on youth development	Participant survey adjusted to include more items related to academics; survey now using pre-post methodology
Qualitative research conducted by program staff through parent focus groups and staff interviews	Responsibility for qualitative research increasingly placed on program staff while evaluators focused on academic analyses; when this was not the case, evaluators played greater role in qualitative research

agency CEO promoted evaluation throughout the organization, (2) the agency invested in internal data systems, (3) all staff were assigned an evaluation role and received relevant orientation, (4) the agency and evaluator designed the evaluation plan together, (5) the agency and evaluator communicated at least once monthly on issues and progress, (6) the evaluator refined processes each year in response to lessons learned and staff input, and (7) the evaluator met with field staff once a year to discuss results.

Though the external evaluator collaborated with WR in designing the general evaluation plan, many aspects of the evaluation were carried out by WR staff, as described in prior sections of this chapter. In addition, WR's internal data department entered individual-level information in an Access database that was designed with the assistance of their evaluator. These data were then exported to the evaluator, who cleaned and merged the data and then conducted the analyses. By sharing the data responsibilities in this way, external evaluators reduced the budget while allowing the program to have direct access to information needed daily, such as enrollment and attendance rate. District data were obtained by the program through collaborative relationships with school districts and with the technical support of the evaluator.

Woodcraft had always conducted staff training with a focus on staff's role working with children. Increasingly, the staff training materials included information on data collection and evaluation. For example, after NCLB, the training binder for new staff presented an overview of evaluation—why it was conducted, what tools were used, how they were administered, and how the information was used to improve the program. As the pressure to produce high-quality, rigorous evaluation increased each year, so did the need to increase the Woodcraft staff's understanding of evaluation, their role in administering student surveys, and knowing how to interpret evaluation findings. Each year, the evaluators facilitated a meeting with the site coordinators to review the evaluation report and key findings. The intention was to gain staff buy-in for their role in the evaluation and create an opportunity to talk in more depth about the evaluation for program improvement. The meetings also enabled staff to examine results of academic impact that could be shared with principals to strengthen their relationship with the schools. A one-page summary of the report was created that each site coordinator could share with principals, placing an emphasis on academic outcomes. Woodcraft also started hosting an annual breakfast with principals from all participating sites to thank them for their collaboration. A summary of the latest evaluation was presented to principals, and they were engaged in discussion regarding lessons learned, challenges, and best practices that could be shared across school sites. These shifts in roles and responsibilities are listed in Table 5.4.

Program Improvement. Evaluation reports were designed to furnish detailed findings while also highlighting how to use the data for program improvement. The findings indicated academic outcomes were not attained

Table 5.4. Division of Evaluation Responsibilities

Division of Evaluation Responsibilities Between Program Staff and Evaluator, Pre-NCLB	Adjustments Made to Division of Evaluation Responsibilities Between Program Staff and Evaluator Influenced by NCLB
Minimal evaluation conducted so roles for program staff were limited	Program staff and evaluators shared roles in evaluation activities and staff training
Evaluation results primarily shared with funders and WR leadership	Evaluator also shared findings with field staff and field staff shared findings with school principals

without a high retention rate. From these findings and the pressure placed on school-linked programs to do more direct academic work, Woodcraft made programmatic adjustments, including using more formal curricula for the clubs and strategies for participant retention. One of the general changes observed since NCLB legislation was a shift in the type of out-of-school-time programs offered on school campuses. A recent study by the Center on Education Policy (2005) described a narrowing of the school curriculum to increase instruction time in math and reading by decreasing time spent on other subjects and enrichment activities. Though not as dramatic, a similar trend was observed in after-school programs. Although WR did not change its primary focus, it did incorporate formal curriculum into their clubs. The

Table 5.5. Program Improvement Efforts

Evaluation Findings	Resultant Programmatic Changes
Participants who attended more often had higher academic scores than those who participated less often *combined with* Participants were not consistently significantly different from nonparticipants in all of these areas	• Researched and purchased curriculum and trained staff on its use to increase integration of after-school math and literacy materials into the program • Added new positions—activities consultants— to provide ongoing expertise, coaching, and support in curriculum development for club leaders

Students who participated for longer periods of time improved more than those who participated less often *combined with* Students' average length of participation is 5–6 months	• Added incentives to increase student retention:
	   – Created an incentive program based on program attendance
	   – Built-in program enhancements of interest to youth (competitions, traveling specialists)

Middle school participants do not stay in WR within a given year as long as elementary participants	• Began MS youth retreats • Started structured incentive program • Expanded and formalized sports leagues and competitions • Restructured MS program so fewer sites assigned to each manager

NEW DIRECTIONS FOR EVALUATION • DOI: 10.1002/ev

curriculum promoted literacy and math skills through a "disguised learning" approach to increase the impact on academic performance. Table 5.5 gives several examples of how the program used outcome data for process purposes.

Conclusion

This focus on long-term academic outcomes might be referred to as a climate change that has affected not only schools directly under NCLB, but also, programs that are school-linked. The tenor of the debate in the American Evaluation Association regarding randomized control trials has certainly had a wide impact on evaluation within educational community-based programs. It has fueled the foundation world's increasingly strong focus on outcome-based measures and increased the pressure on evaluation practitioners to educate clients on long-term outcomes, particularly academic achievement. There has been an increase in the number of community-based organizations that feel the need to measure academic outcomes regardless of the nature of their programs. Thus, evaluators are often requested by clients to measure academic outcomes that are not linked to the goals of the program and for which there are few or no resources to adequately measure them. The WR case study constitutes an example of a program that increased its ability to address this pressure. The WR evaluation does not meet the SBR ideal, but the adjustments made have improved both the program and its evaluation.

Woodcraft is an example of how a community-based organization with school-linked programming has acknowledged, and responded to, changes in the school environment brought on by the NCLB legislation. Consequently, WR made appropriate programmatic enhancements to address the changing needs of schools and school administrators even though the program itself did not fall directly under NCLB. These enhancements have strengthened the program's relationship with schools and school districts. Woodcraft also had to make changes to its evaluation plan and instruments to demonstrate relevance to the schools, including how it can contribute specifically to improvement in student academic performance. These changes have been influenced by the NCLB evaluation guidelines and required close collaboration among the program, its local evaluator, and partner schools.

References

Center on Education Policy. (2005). *NCLB Policy Brief 3*. Washington, DC: Author. Retrieved March 28, 2007, from http://www.cepdc.org/document/docWindow.cfm? fuseaction=document.viewDocument&documentid=51&documentFormatId=686

Gomby, D. S., & Larson, C. S. (1992). Evaluation of school-linked services. In R. Behrman (Ed.), *The future of children: School linked services*, (pp. 68–84). Los Altos, CA: Center for the Future of Children and David and Lucile Packard Foundation.

Greene, J. C., Caracelli, V., & Graham, W. F. (1989). Toward a conceptual framework for multimethod evaluation designs. *Educational Evaluation and Policy Analysis, 11*, 255–274.

Kane, T. (2004). *The impact of after school programs: Interpreting the results of four recent evaluations* (working paper). New York: W. T. Grant Foundation.

Lodestar Management/Research. (2005). *Woodcraft Rangers annual evaluation report for 2003–04: Elementary and Middle School Programs.* Los Angeles: Author.

Lodestar Management/Research. (2006). *Woodcraft Rangers process evaluation report: Key factors related to program recruitment, retention and outcomes.* Los Angeles: Author.

Nichols, S., Glass, G., & Berliner, D. (2005). *High-stakes testing and student achievement: Problems for the No Child Left Behind Act.* Education Policy Studies Laboratory. Retrieved April 26, 2007, from http://epsl.asu.edu/epru/epru_2005_ Research_ Writing.htm

No Child Left Behind Act. (2001). Public Law No. 107–110. 107th Congress, 110 *Congressional Record* 1425, 115 Stat.

Pratt, C., McGuigan, W., & Katzev, A. (2005). Measuring program outcomes: Using retrospective pretest methodology. *American Journal of Evaluation, 21*, 341–349.

U.S. Department of Education. (2003). Notice of proposed priority: Scientifically based evaluation methods (RIN 1890-ZA00). *Federal Register, 68*(213), 62445–62447.

BLANCA FLOR GUILLÉN-WOODS *is an independent consultant based in Washington, DC, and former senior research associate at Lodestar Management/Research.*

MONICA A. KAISER *is vice president of the Kaiser Group, a company that supports nonprofit organizations in achieving their mission.*

MAURA J. HARRINGTON *is the vice president of consulting services and senior researcher at Lodestar Management/Research.*

NEW DIRECTIONS FOR EVALUATION • DOI: 10.1002/ev

Azin, M., & Resendez, M. G. (2008). Measuring student progress: Changes and challenges under No Child Left Behind. In T. Berry & R. M. Eddy (Eds.), *Consequences of No Child Left Behind for educational evaluation. New Directions for Evaluation, 117,* 71–84.

6

Measuring Student Progress: Changes and Challenges Under No Child Left Behind

Mariam Azin, Miriam G. Resendez

Abstract

Evaluators face a number of challenges in using student assessment data, given varying state and federal accountability requirements. Approaches to measuring student progress and specific characteristics of state assessment systems influence how data can be used. The continuous changes to state assessment systems and data create a significant challenge for evaluators wishing to use state repositories of student achievement data over time to track changes in achievement. The authors discuss the larger questions of the validity of tests being used and the potential limitations of single measures of student achievement in using state-collected student assessment data. © Wiley Periodicals, Inc.

U nder No Child Left Behind (NCLB, 2001), states are required to measure school performance toward Adequate Yearly Progress (AYP). Complying with AYP requirements has had a substantial impact on states' accountability systems. For example, large-scale testing has become ubiquitous as states sought to meet the 2005–2006 deadline that required them to administer reading and language arts and math assessments to

NEW DIRECTIONS FOR EVALUATION, no. 117, Spring 2008 © Wiley Periodicals, Inc.
Published online in Wiley InterScience (www.interscience.wiley.com) • DOI: 10.1002/ev.253

students in grades 3 to 8 and once during high school. By the 2007–2008 school year, states must also administer science assessments at least three times during a student's academic career. Of course, these large-scale accountability systems do not come without cost; indeed, the Government Accounting Office (GAO, 2003) estimated that with the current mix of tests used by states, costs associated with the NCLB testing requirement are likely to be close to $4 billion.

The increased availability and emphasis being placed on student performance data has implications for evaluators. Certainly, an intended purpose of NCLB was to promote accountability by holding local and state education agencies responsible for meeting performance targets for *all* students. In addition, NCLB has increased the level of uniformity across states in terms of the content (mathematics, reading, science) and grade level being assessed, as well as the frequency with which such assessment is occurring. Still, there has been considerable variation across states in terms of how federal accountability requirements translate into practice. Hence, the state accountability systems that have emerged can present real challenges to researchers and evaluators working within the educational milieu of NCLB.

To what extent can evaluators draw on state assessment data as part of educational evaluations? What factors need to be taken into consideration? Certainly, a plethora of assessment data are potentially available as outcome measures. The focus of this chapter is to examine the critical issues in assessment of student progress as a result of NCLB. In particular, we focus on how such data can potentially be used by evaluators in the post-NCLB era. The chapter begins with a discussion of the varied approaches being taken to measure student progress and how such methods can influence the conclusions being made. This is followed by an overview of the characteristics of state assessment systems and how such features influence the ways in which data can be used. This chapter concludes with a summary of how evaluators can navigate the challenges associated with using state assessment data for purposes of educational evaluation. Included under this heading is a brief discussion of why evaluators may want to draw on existing state assessment data as a resource, particularly given the significance that this outcome measure has taken on in the mind of many educators operating under the accountability umbrella of NCLB.

Measuring Student Progress

In examining student progress under NCLB, it is critical for evaluators and educators to consider the method being used to determine progress. Currently, a potpourri of methods are used by states to measure student progress and calculate AYP. Generally, they can be categorized as status models, improvement models, and growth models (including value-added models). The differences across these methods for calculating change in student performance are noteworthy and have major implications for how progress is interpreted, and for the validity of those interpretations.

Status Models. The AYP model is a status model. It looks at students' performance during a specific year (or average across multiple years) and compares this value with a preestablished target (the Annual Measurable Objective, AMO, under NCLB). The problems associated with status models have been discussed extensively elsewhere (see Novak & Fuller, 2003; and Goldschmidt & Choi, 2007). To summarize, this model has several limitations, including, but not limited to, (1) not fully capturing student performance on the basis of cut scores, thereby risking the possible misclassification of those students near cut points; (2) placing schools with more subgroup representation at a disadvantage because they have more targets to meet; (3) being highly sensitive to the characteristics of students enrolled in the school as opposed to how the school teaches its students (for example, a school with a large influx of English language learners, or ELLs, will likely show lower performance than a school with a very small proportion of incoming ELLs); and (4) failing to account for a student's unique educational history. With this in mind, evaluators should be cautious in using AYP status as an indicator of success or lack thereof, given flaws inherent in this procedure.

Improvement Models. The improvement model can be differentiated from the status model by its focus on changes between groups of students (for example, third graders in 2004 and third graders in 2005). A concrete example of an improvement model is NCLB's Safe Harbor provision. Under Safe Harbor, a subgroup that fails to make AYP under the status model can still make AYP if the number of students who score below proficiency is reduced by 10% compared to the previous year's group. Thus, the focus is on improving the performance for a subgroup of students. However, improvement models do not indicate anything about individual student growth in academic performance. Further, like the status model, this one is also sensitive to the type of student enrolled at a particular point in time.

Growth Models. In contrast to the status model being used by states to calculate AYP, growth models can be defined as measuring changes in performance (proficiency level, test scores) for a specific unit (students, classes, schools, and so on) for 2 or more years. There has been interest recently in growth models among education policy makers. According to a recent report from the GAO (2006), as of March 2006 26 states reported using growth models in addition to the AYP status model. Of those not currently implementing, 22 were considering or were in the process of implementing growth models. In addition, the U.S. Department of Education recently implemented the Growth Model Pilot Program, allowing states to submit plans to use "high-quality" growth models in their AYP calculations (U.S. Department of Education, 2006). This increased interest in growth models is due, in part, to increased recognition that alternatives or supplemental models are needed to make more informed educational decisions.

Indeed, there are several advantages to growth models as opposed to status models. The former typically depend on data that (1) is vertically scaled (that is, across-grade scores on a single scale permits continuous tracking of students as they progress from one grade to the next), (2) can be linked to individual students or schools over time, and (3) may employ more sophisticated techniques (for instance, hierarchical linear modeling). Growth models tend to account for extraneous variables that may lead to incorrect conclusions about a school's effectiveness (Yu, Kennedy, Teddlie, & Crain, 2007). Furthermore, using individual student data, including students' prior performance, permits more accurate estimates of student performance. From a policy perspective:

> Growth models can provide states with more detailed information on how schools' and students' performance has changed from year to year. Growth models can recognize schools whose students are making significant gains on state tests but are still not proficient and may provide incentives for schools with mostly proficient students to make greater improvements. Educators can use the growth models of individual students to tailor interventions to the needs of particular students or groups. In this respect, models that measure individual students' growth provide the most in-depth and useful information, yet most of the models currently in use are not designed to do this. (GAO, 2006, p. 33)

It is beyond the scope of this chapter to consider all the available growth models in detail; here, we briefly describe a sampling of growth models that are being used in states as part of their state accountability systems, including those proposed for the Growth Model Pilot Program. It should be noted that although all of the growth models here share the feature of measuring changes in performance, as will be discussed they vary in their level of precision in measuring student progress.

The simplest form of growth models are those based on *gain scores*. They are relatively simple to compute; the gain score is calculated by obtaining the difference in the starting point and an endpoint. Gain scores can be calculated at the individual level or aggregated at the school or district level. A disadvantage associated with gain-score models is that even though they are easier to compute, they are less precise than more sophisticated growth models in explaining change in student performance.

Expected growth and *value tables* are growth models that have been proposed under the Growth Model Pilot Program (Goldschmidt & Choi, 2007). The expected growth model involves predicting individual student performance on the basis of current or past performance. This value is then compared to a target for AYP purposes. Value tables track student growth at the standard performance level, with points allocated according to student movement among proficiency levels from year to year. These models tend to be easy to communicate and do not require vertically scaled scores. However, there are disadvantages. As a result of federal guidelines, they do not take into account student- and school-level characteristics, which can place "potentially unobtainable expectations for growth on initially poor performing students, as well as placing different growth goals for initially poor performing students compared with students initially performing well" (Goldschmidt & Choi, 2007, p. 8). In addition, focusing on each student's growth and not allowing aggregation of growth parameters means these estimates may not be precise.

In contrast to the aforementioned models, the *value-added* approach explicitly includes in the model student demographic characteristics, school characteristics, prior achievement, and other important variables related to achievement. As such, value-added models can potentially isolate the effects of teachers and schools from other factors not related to school (as with family or peer influences). In addition, research shows a large variation in teacher effectiveness, and to the extent that characteristics of teachers are linked to student performance, this information can help target areas needing improvement (McCaffrey, Lockwood, Koretz, Louis, & Hamilton, 2004). Although the potential benefits are great, there are disadvantages to using these models. For example, whether the model can adequately distinguish the effects of a teacher has come into question (Goldschmidt et al., 2005). Further, these models tend to be complex and results can be difficult to interpret. Data and computing requirements are also often substantial.

Another type of growth model is the *multilevel* (or *hierarchical linear*) model, which measures both student- and group-level growth. By examining performance at multiple levels, it is possible to examine how growth is related, for example, to teacher- and school-level factors. Other advantages of these models are that they account for nesting effects (students within classes within schools), can handle nonlinear growth, and have been found to be more precise in growth estimates than gain score or ordinary least squares regression models (Tong & O'Malley, 2006). Further, this model tends to be more flexible in its ability to handle missing and unbalanced data (Raudenbush & Bryk, 2002). However, these models also can be complex, making model specification and interpretation of results difficult.

In summary, there are various approaches being used by states for measuring student progress, from simple status models currently employed by all states in determining AYP to more complex growth models, such as the value-added (as in Tennessee). Further, the post-NCLB environment has seen an increase in use of alternatives, such as growth models for measuring student progress. Their use has spurred the availability of data linked to individual students and comparable across grades. Along with the changes that many states have made in their accountability systems, this has profound implications for evaluators considering using state assessment data.

NEW DIRECTIONS FOR EVALUATION • DOI: 10.1002/ev

Using State Assessment Data in Evaluations

In light of the tremendous amount of resources spent to create this vast repository of data, evaluators would be remiss not to consider the possibility of using state assessment data. Indeed, there are several reasons for researchers conducting educational evaluations to consider drawing on state assessment data as a potential measure[1] in their studies. First, it is available, requiring no actual data collection. Thus there is no additional testing time for students and evaluation costs are generally reduced by eliminating the need to purchase and score assessments. Drawing on existing state assessment data as part of a battery of outcome measures could also potentially enhance the sensitivity of an evaluation. Moreover, the data which exist can oftentimes permit longitudinal analyses of performance trends over time— an endeavor that can be very time-consuming and costly if one seeks to undertake it from scratch. Similarly, depending on the nature of the intervention and sampling frame employed, evaluators can often gain access to large sample sizes that make analyses sensitive to detecting the small effects typical of educational settings. Finally, given the importance placed on how students perform on state assessments, these measures can be highly meaningful in the minds of educators and other stakeholders associated with an evaluation effort.

Considering the appropriateness, feasibility, and practicality of using existing state assessment data, however, one must take into account several factors. First, it is important to keep in mind that the flexibility built into NCLB gives states latitude in terms of how they measure student performance and how they define and calculate AYP. As a result, there is considerable variation across state assessments in terms of (1) type, quality, and difficulty; (2) alignment to state standards; (3) established proficiency level or cut scores (and the processes used to determine them); (4) the type of score produced; and (5) the comparability of such scores over time and cohorts of students (Chudowsky & Chudowsky, 2007).

For example, we have conducted archival studies using existing state assessment data across four disparate states (California, Georgia, South Carolina, and Texas; Resendez, Fahmy, & Manley, 2004; Resendez, Sridharan, & Azin, 2005, 2007a, 2007b). These archival studies involved obtaining state assessment data to examine performance trends over time among students in schools before, during, and after introduction of an educational program. As Table 6.1 shows, there is a great deal of variability across these four states in terms of the type of assessment used, the years and grade levels assessed, type of score produced, comparability of scores and assessments over time, and level of data that can be obtained. All of these factors had profound implications for which types of analysis could or could not be conducted using these data.

As is clearly shown in the table, the changes constantly being made to accountability models, including assessment and grade level tested, makes

Table 6.1. Data Characteristics: Examples From Four States

	California			Texas		Georgia	South Carolina
Assessments[a]	California Standards Test	California Achievement Test 6	Stanford 9	Texas Assessment of Academic Skills	Texas Assessment of Knowledge and Skills	Georgia's Criterion-Referenced Competency Test	Palmetto Achievement Challenge Tests
Grade levels and years of assessment data available	Grades 2–8; although began in 1998, data available only from 2002 to 2006	Grades 2–8 from 2003–2004; since 2005, administered in Grades 3 and 7	Grades 2–8 from 1998 to 2002	Grades 3, 5, 7 from 1990 to 1993; Grades 3–8 from 1994 to 2002	Grades 3–8 from 2003 to present	Grades 4, 6, 8 in 2000, 2001, and 2003; Grades 1–8 in 2002, and 2004–2006	Grades 3–8; although began in 1999, data available only from 2002 to present
Assessment Type[b]	CRT	NRT	NRT	CRT	CRT	CRT	CRT
Scores available	Proficiency level and scale score	Scale scores; percentile ranking; normal curve equivalent	Scale scores; percentile ranking; normal curve equivalent	Texas Learning Index; Objective mastery and percentage correct on each objective, whether or not a student met the minimum expectations for the test	TAKS scale score; whether or not a student met the subject standard; percentage correct on each objective	Mean CRCT score (aggregated); percentage of students within schools meeting or exceeding math objectives	Scale score and proficiency level
Assessments equated	No		Yes	No		N/A	N/A
Level of data	Individual, without identifiers			Individual, with scrubbed identifiers		School	Individual, with scrubbed identifiers
Vertically scaled	No	Yes	Yes	Yes	No	No	Yes

[a]Our evaluations focused on elementary and middle school math performance; as such, the table excludes data that may be available at the high school level or alternative assessments.

[b]CRT = criterion-referenced test; NRT = norm-referenced test.

measurement of student progress increasingly difficult and complex. If a change in test occurs, then student scores on the new test cannot be compared with scores on the previous test unless the two are equated. Moreover, even if the same assessment is used across grade levels, if the scores are not vertically scaled, then one cannot compare assessment results for a given student as he or she progresses into higher grade levels (that is, individual student growth analysis).

Measuring growth longitudinally across grade levels can be similarly challenging given the types of scores often produced by criterion-referenced tests (CRTs) or standards-based assessments being used by states for purposes of calculating AYP. They include proficiency level (that is, novice, below proficient, proficient, advanced) and nondevelopmental scale scores. Such scores, though conducive to cross-sectional analyses in which comparisons are made among similar groups of students (for example, improvement models), make individual growth analyses less precise and problematic. However, some state CRTs, such as Georgia's Palmetto Achievement Challenge Test and the Texas Assessment of Academic Skills, which were designed with measuring student growth in mind, yield developmentally scaled scores in addition to proficiency level.

Additionally, the type of score produced and released has implications for the sensitivity of analysis in detecting changes or effects. Scale scores are more sensitive to change than categorical proficiency levels. Nevertheless, an analysis conducted using proficiency cut points is often more meaningful and easily communicated, because such results can speak to a threshold of performance that has taken on increasing importance in the mind of educators over recent years. Additionally, some states produce subscale scores, for example, across strands of mathematics performance, which enables more minute examination of effects compared to the information supplied with total or overall scores.

Inconsistency in student identifiers used can also present yet another obstacle to measuring individual student progress over time. For example, in South Carolina, student identifiers have not been used consistently through the years. A statewide system is being implemented, but this has not always been the case. As such, matching via individual student identifiers is problematic. Indeed, for matching of students on longitudinal data using data prior to statewide adoption of student identifiers, the state relies on algorithms using a combination of student and school characteristics. This method becomes difficult as heterogeneity in the student population increases.

Further, it is also important to keep in mind that state standards and thresholds for proficiency can differ dramatically across states. Data from the National Assessment of Educational Progress (NAEP) shows evidence of this:

In 2003, 34% of Colorado students scored proficient or above on NAEP compared to 28% for Missouri. But on their own state tests in 2003, 67% of Colorado students scored proficient or above compared to just 21.3% in Missouri. The difference between 67% and 21.3% clearly has more to do with how rigorously states set their performance standards than with real differences in achievement between students. (Linn, 2005, p. 6)

The question comes to mind as to whether differences in student progress are due to actual changes in student attainment of knowledge and skills or rather what the state interprets as a sufficient threshold of performance. To the extent that an evaluation involves conducting analyses within a single state that has maintained a common metric for determining proficiency over time, this may not really be an issue. However, if one looks at making comparisons across states, then comparability is problematic because proficiency standards can vary substantially from state to state. For instance, by fall 2004, 47 states had asked the U.S. Department of Education to allow them to make changes to their NCLB accountability plans—changes that, in many cases, consisted of a difference in how proficiency was determined (Chudowsky, Chudowsky, Kober, & Stark-Rentner, 2004).

Although many of these data characteristics are well documented and can be readily detected, the issue of the extent to which subpopulations are accurately identified and coded on state assessment data is more of an unknown. For example, in our recent archival study using California assessment data, analysis on students who were of limited English proficiency (LEP) was limited thanks to changes in criteria and categorization over time. Moreover, a large number of students simply had missing values for this variable. As another example, free- and reduced-price lunch status tends to be identified far more frequently at the elementary level compared to upper grade levels. Furthermore, identification of "at-risk" students is notoriously unreliable because the extent to which such students are identified within schools varies tremendously.

Yet another factor to consider is that if one is seeking to access state assessment data from a state department of education rather than a district or school directly, then it is necessary to find out how the state has interpreted the Family Educational Rights and Privacy Act (FERPA), a federal law that regulates release of children's educational records. Unsurprisingly, there is tremendous variability in this regard as well. Some states (such as Texas and South Carolina) "scrub" the identification numbers of students, so that even though researchers never have access to the true student ID, the same made-up ID is used for a given student across multiple assessment years. Such a method makes it possible for researchers to conduct longitudinal *student-level* analysis, looking at student performance trends over time (before, during, and after introduction of a given intervention). However, other states release only school-level data (an example is Georgia). Still others furnish student-level data without IDs so that these students cannot be matched over time (as with California). In sum, though most analysts of FERPA law conclude that are certainly ways for state assessment data to be released to researchers such that individual students cannot be identified (King, Schexnayder, & Gourgey, 2005), ultimately whether and how this is done is determined at the state level.

Practical Implications for Evaluators

As noted, the characteristics of the assessment data available determine what types of analyses are possible as well as contribute to the ensuing discussion on study limitations. For example, once the characteristics of the state assessment data within the four previously mentioned states were identified, we could determine both our sampling frame and the analyses that could be conducted. Here are examples of strategies that can be used to address the limitations of data obtained from state assessments:

- If analysis is prohibitive at the student level, then consider obtaining data at the school level. Given the higher level of analyses that must be conducted, however, a larger sample of schools is likely to be needed to achieve sufficient power.
- If scores are not vertically scaled or student identifiers are not available such that growth cannot be measured on an individual level over time, consider conducting cross-sectional analysis as opposed to longitudinal cohort analysis. For example, for the evaluation using California statewide assessment data, students at a certain grade level were compared to students at the same grade level during other school years (fourth graders in 2002 through 2006). Because the intervention of interest was during a specific year within this time interval (say, in 2004), it was possible to examine whether there was a change in performance following implementation of the program. Strong conclusions are problematic, but this method still allows valuable information to be obtained with regard to the intervention of interest.
- To increase the sensitivity of analyses, consider using multiple outcome measures available from the state. For example, as noted, some states make available total scale scores in addition to proficiency level and scores on various objectives within an academic domain. By supplying results from multiple types of measures, one can reach a greater audience and provide meaningful information for numerous stakeholders.
- If conducting a study in which comparisons will be made between groups (such as a quasi-experimental design), consider increasing the comparability of students and schools from the outset. For example, as part of the state accountability system, Texas conducts its own matching in which comparison sites are matched to a target campus on the basis of

school-level characteristics (percentage of students in various ethnic categories, percentage ELL, and so on). Because matching was already conducted by the state, we were able to take advantage of this information to select comparison sites. In contrast, in our evaluation of a math curriculum in the state of Georgia we employed propensity matching procedures to match schools according to important characteristics of the student population (enrollment, ethnicity distribution, ELL distribution, disability distribution, and so forth). This procedure allowed us to obtain highly comparable schools in our sample that were virtually equivalent in terms of student composition.

The focus of this chapter is on the possibilities and challenges posed to evaluators who are pondering use of state assessment data as a potential data source. But there are some central conceptual issues that, even if beyond the scope of this single chapter, must nonetheless be given due consideration by evaluators drawing on state assessment data:

- There are substantive issues around the validity of the tests being used that must be acknowledged, in particular as they relate to testing students within certain subpopulations, such as LEP and special education students. Recent changes made by the U.S. Department of Education (2004) have alleviated some of these concerns.[2] Still, there continue to be fundamental issues with regard to testing of students in these special populations that need to be considered. For example, research shows that ELL students do more poorly on longer test items regardless of the level of difficulty because of the language demands embedded within these longer items (Abedi, 2002).
- Due consideration must always be given to the content of the assessments being used, what constructs they are measuring, and how they are measuring them. Are they valid and reliable? To what extent are they aligned to the outcomes of the program being evaluated? Is this measure sensitive to picking up the effects associated with the intervention of interest? At what point is it realistic to expect changes to manifest themselves in terms of student performance? For example, in evaluating a professional development initiative, evaluators should examine changes in teacher knowledge and practices before expecting to see changes in student performance. It could be argued that the post-NCLB era has promoted a climate of unrealistic expectations in regard to how soon one might expect to see results in terms of student achievement.
- In light of the limitations inherent within any single measure, good evaluation practice always points to use of multiple outcome measures whenever possible. To the extent that state assessment data exist and are available as another measure, they can be used as such; but in our opinion a single assessment should never be considered as "the measure"

(we recognize that this is at odds with how AYP is currently being done in many states). Indeed, whenever inordinate emphasis is placed on a single indicator of success, the phenomenon of interest is invariably affected—and not necessarily for the better. For example, with the emphasis on state testing that has come as a result of NCLB, schools are spending more time on reading, math, and test preparation. Given that the amount of classroom instructional time is fixed, the changes in instructional emphasis as a result of teaching to the test is inevitably coming at the expense of other subject areas, skills, and concepts that, though important, may not be reflected in state standards or the assessment (Jennings & Stark-Rentner, 2006).

- If the study design involves drawing on state assessment data for retrospective analysis, the archival nature of such a study usually means there is a lack of implementation data. This makes it difficult to explain how or why evaluators are seeing the performance trends that are emerging. Such limitations need to be openly discussed in any study of this nature. Of course, if one is considering using state assessment data as part of a prospective study, steps can be taken to employ measures of implementation so that the context and nature of intervention of interest is adequately measured and described.

Conclusion

Evaluations on the effectiveness of educational interventions continue to be critically important as schools try to select interventions that can significantly improve the knowledge and skills of students. Given the complexity of the educational phenomenon we are examining, it is necessary to draw on the full arsenal of resources at our disposal to try to gain insight into the phenomenon of interest. Any single study or data source will have inherent limitations, but the cumulative body of knowledge and research becomes far more compelling over time. Studies and analyses involving state assessment data merely draw on one more tool that is potentially at our disposal. Furthermore, to make sure our work is relevant to stakeholders, it is necessary to recognize the context in which they are operating. It is undeniable that, as a result of NCLB, performance on state assessments has become increasingly important.

Notes

1. Although we are discussing the potential for using state assessment data as an outcome measure, we are not advocating its use as the only outcome measure. As is discussed, there are many limitations associated with state assessment data that should be acknowledged. Furthermore, multiple assessment and outcome measures are generally desirable in any evaluation in order to enhance the sensitivity of the study and help compensate for limitations inherent within any single assessment.

New Directions for Evaluation • DOI: 10.1002/ev

2. This includes allowing states to increase the percent of students with disabilities who can be tested against "modified" state standards and allowing states, for up to 2 years, to include students who have attained proficiency in the LEP subgroup.

References

Abedi, J. (2002). Assessment and accommodations of English language: Issues, concerns and recommendations. *Journal of School Improvement, 3.* Retrieved March 2007, from http://www.icsac.org/jsi/2002v3i1/assessment

Chudowsky, N., & Chudowsky, V. (2007, January). *No Child Left Behind at five: A review of changes to state accountability plans.* Washington, DC: Center on Education Policy.

Chudowsky, N., Chudowsky, V., Kober, N., & Stark-Rentner, D. (2004, October). *Rule changes could help more schools meet test score targets for the No Child Left Behind Act.* Washington, DC: Center on Education Policy.

Goldschmidt, P., & Choi, K. (2007, Spring). *The practical benefits of growth models for accountability and the limitations under NCLB* (CRESST Policy Brief 9). Los Angeles: University of California, Center for Research on Evaluation, Standards, and Student Testing.

Goldschmidt, P., Roschewski, P., Choi, K., Auty, W., Hebbler, S., Blank, R., et al. (2005, October). *Policymakers guide to growth models for school accountability: How do accountability models differ?* Los Angeles: University of California, Center for Research on Evaluation, Standards, and Student Testing.

Jennings, J., & Stark-Rentner, D. (2006). *Ten big effects of the No Child Left Behind Act on public schools.* Washington, DC: Center on Education Policy.

King, C. T., Schexnayder, D. T., & Gourgey, H. (2005). *Beyond the numbers: Improving postsecondary success through a central Texas high school data center* (Policy Research Report Number 148). Austin: University of Texas, Lyndon B. Johnson School of Public Affairs.

Linn, R. L. (2005, Summer). *Fixing the NCLB accountability system* (CRESST Policy Brief 8). Los Angeles: University of California, Center for Research on Evaluation, Standards, and Student Testing.

McCaffrey, D. F., Lockwood, J., Koretz, D., Louis, T. A., & Hamilton, L. (2004). Models for value-added modeling of teacher effects. *Journal of Educational and Behavioral Statistics, 29,* 67–101.

No Child Left Behind Act. (2001). Public Law No. 107–110. 107th Congress, 110 *Congressional Record,* 1425, 115 Stat.

Novak, J., & Fuller, B. (2003). *Penalizing diverse schools? Similar test scores, but different students, bring federal sanction* (PACE Policy Brief). Berkeley: Policy Analysis for California Education.

Raudenbush, S. W., & Bryk, A. S. (2002). *Hierarchical linear models* (2nd ed.). Thousand Oaks, CA: Sage.

Resendez, M., Fahmy, A., & Manley, M. (2004). The relationship between using Saxon Math and student performance on Texas statewide assessments. Jackson, WY: PRES Associates.

Resendez, M., Sridharan, S., & Azin, M. (2005). The relationship between using Saxon Elementary and Middle School Math and student performance on Georgia statewide assessments. Jackson, WY: PRES Associates.

Resendez, M., Sridharan, S., & Azin, M. (2007a). The relationship between using Saxon Elementary and Middle School Math and student performance on California statewide assessments. Jackson, WY: PRES Associates.

Resendez, M., Sridharan, S., & Azin, M. (2007b). The relationship between using Saxon Elementary and Middle School Math and student performance on South Carolina statewide assessments. Jackson, WY: PRES Associates.

Tong, Y., & O'Malley, K. (2006). *An empirical investigation of growth models.* Pearson Educational Measurement. Retrieved March 2007, from http://www.pearsone dmeasurement.com/research/research.htm

U.S. Department of Education. (2004, February). *Secretary Paige announces new policies to help English Language Learners.* Retrieved March 2007, from http://www.ed.gov/ news/pressreleases/2004/02/02192004.html

U.S. Department of Education. (2006, January). *Peer review guidance for the NCLB Growth Model Pilot applications.* Retrieved March 2007, from http://www. ed.gov/ policy/elsec/guid/growthmodelguidance.pdf

U.S. Government Accounting Office. (2003). *Title I: Characteristics of tests will influence expenses; information sharing may help states realize efficiencies* (GAO Publication No. 06–815). Washington, DC: Author.

U.S. Government Accountability Office. (2006). *States face challenges measuring academic growth that education's initiatives may help address* (GAO Publication No. 06–661). Washington, DC: Author.

Yu, F., Kennedy, E., Teddlie, C., & Crain, M. (2007). *Identifying effective and ineffective schools for accountability purposes: A comparison of four generic types of accountability models.* Retrieved March 2007, from http://www.ccsso.org/content/pdfs/Revised% 20byYu%20Kennedy%20Teddlie%20Crain.doc

MARIAM AZIN is the president of Planning, Research, and Evaluation Services (PRES Associates).

MIRIAM G. RESENDEZ is the director of research and evaluation at PRES Associates.

Baughman, M. (2008). The influence of scientific research and evaluation on publishing educational curriculum. In T. Berry & R. M. Eddy (Eds.), *Consequences of No Child Left Behind for educational evaluation. New Directions for Evaluation, 117,* 85–94.

7

The Influence of Scientific Research and Evaluation on Publishing Educational Curriculum

Marcy Baughman

Abstract

Prior to the No Child Left Behind (NCLB) Act, scientific research to support development of curriculum materials or to demonstrate curricular efficacy was not required. NCLB transformed the development and publishing process for K–12 educational materials by prompting publishers to increase funding for experimentally based research on educational products used in schools. To maintain a viable place in the market, textbook publishers have faced challenges such as difficulty in conducting experimental research in schools, coordination with states' proposed curriculum adoption cycles, and use of limited resources to meet the needs of many more stakeholders in the new accountability framework. © Wiley Periodicals, Inc.

The No Child Left Behind Act (NCLB, 2001) transformed the development and publishing process for K–12 educational materials. Prior to NCLB, scientific research to support program development or demonstrate program efficacy (all educational curriculum and materials will be referred to as "programs") was not required, and some viewed it

New Directions for Evaluation, no. 117, Spring 2008 © Wiley Periodicals, Inc.
Published online in Wiley InterScience (www.interscience.wiley.com) • DOI: 10.1002/ev.254

as a value-added component to program development. However, NCLB mandates use of scientific research to "prove" the effectiveness of curricular materials. As a result of this directive, textbook publishers responded with an abrupt increase in funding to (1) continue enhancing the development of curricular materials through use of solid, empirical research and (2) initiate a program of experimental research on their program in schools. However, implementing these changes has come with great challenges, notably, difficulty in conducting experimental research in schools, timing the research along with the states' proposed adoption cycles, and using research to meet the needs of a diverse group of stakeholders invested in producing high-quality curricula for students. This chapter explores how the key drivers associated with NCLB have an impact on the textbook-publishing process as well as the complexities that have arisen as a result of these driving influences.

Driving Influences Associated With NCLB

There are three main "drivers" associated with NCLB that have affected the publishing process: the What Works Clearinghouse, textbook adoption requirements, and scientifically based research (SBR). Although only SBR is specifically mentioned in NCLB, the other two drivers have their roots in the legislation as well. Together, these forces have influenced how textbook publishers operate internally and externally.

What Works Clearinghouse. Under NCLB, publishers needed to create textbooks that were "guaranteed" to increase student achievement and would work with any teacher and any learner. School districts were also required to have this evidence from publishers before considering adoption of their programs, particularly for purchasing with Title I funds. The intention of the U.S. Department of Education's Institute for Educational Sciences (IES) was to have the What Works Clearinghouse (WWC) function as the primary source of information available to states and districts in making decisions about selecting educational curriculum for their schools.

Although other organizations have been developed to expand the scientific research base (for example, the Campbell Corporation and the Center for Data-Driven Reform in Education at Johns Hopkins University), the WWC was specifically established by the IES to give educators, policy makers, researchers, and the public a central and trusted source of scientific evidence of what "works" in education. The WWC's primary focus is on determining whether programs are effective given the quality of research conducted to support this effectiveness. The WWC considers randomized control trials (RCTs) and regression discontinuity designs (without randomization, attrition, or disruption problems) to meet "full evidence standards." Strong quasi-experimental designs that have comparison groups and meet other WWC standards conform to their evidence standards "with reservations" (http://www.w-w-c.org). Other designs do not meet evidence standards and are not reviewed by the WWC, primarily because only strong experimental research can assure educators that any growth in student achievement is the result of the program rather than other, potentially confounding, factors. Though there is ongoing debate in the field regarding the value of what constitutes "evidence" (Donaldson, Christie, & Mark, in press), these designs have continued to remain the optimal choice for efficacy research of published materials.

Textbook Adoption. The added complexity of the textbook adoption process since NCLB has not appeared readily in the evaluation literature, although it has numerous implications for the work of educators and evaluators. To describe the process, textbook adoptions are broken into either state or open territory adoptions. Approximately 20 states use the former. In a state adoption, publishers submit their textbooks for review to the state department of education, and a list of approved products is disseminated to the districts. The districts in these states are allowed to purchase programs only from the approved adoption list. In the remaining 30 states, considered open-territory, districts are able to review the programs for themselves and determine which they will adopt. The responsibility for ensuring that programs have evidence of effectiveness is often at the district level in open-territory states.

Under NCLB, the textbook review process in state and open-territory adoptions now requires that publishers document program effectiveness (although the level of scientific rigor and the documentation required varies by state and district). Publishers are routinely asked to furnish evidence that RCTs have been completed, or are in the process of being completed, in order for that product to be available for adoption in the state. However, the request usually comes in the form of multiple yes-no questions that may fall under a number of headings: systematic and empirical methods, rigorous data analyses, reliable and valid data collection, strong research design, detailed results that allow replication, and results subject to scrutiny. Because it is nearly impossible to answer every question with a simple dichotomous response, addendums are always included. This process can be time-consuming and tedious given that few checklists are standardized across state or districts. One uniform set of standards and expectations for research requirements across states would help to streamline this process for publishers. This would particularly benefit those states or districts without a research office.

Dual Purposes of Scientifically Based Research. The term *scientifically based research* (SBR) is used throughout the NCLB legislation, and described as "research that involves the application of rigorous, systematic, and objective procedures to obtain reliable and valid knowledge relevant to education activities and programs" (DOE, 2005, p. 3587). Although it is reasonable to assume that educational programs are built on scientific research, very few guidelines exist regarding how publishers implement this during development of educational programs. On the other hand, many established guidelines are in place to evaluate the effectiveness of educational programs once they have been developed. It is here that the dual purposes of SBR are clear: (1) ensuring that SBR is used to develop curricula on a sound, scientific base; and (2) documenting that SBR has been used to evaluate program effectiveness. The need to distinguish between these two purposes is clear; Slavin (2002) has argued that "the fact that a program is based on scientific research does not mean that it is in fact effective. For example, imagine an instructional program whose materials are thoroughly based on scientific research, but which is so difficult to implement that in practice teachers do a poor job of it, or which is so boring that students do not pay attention . . ." (p. 19). Differentiating between these two purposes is important because they occur at different phases in program development and have their own implications for publishers.

Another important distinction that arises related to SBR is between efficacy trials and effectiveness trials (Chen, 2005). A study of program effectiveness would emphasize the discovery and explanation of what makes the program work in a typical field setting. It places greater emphasis on external validity and how differences in student achievement or implementation occurred. Studies of program effectiveness occur in a standard classroom setting with all the corresponding factors that may affect the research hypotheses, such as teacher experience, student motivation, time on task, and so forth. By contrast, an efficacy study would occur in a lab-like setting where all factors that could affect student achievement are tightly controlled, which would prevent publishers from generalizing the conclusions to an average user of the program. NCLB legislation stresses the need for studies of program efficacy; however, studies of program effectiveness are more frequently funded by publishers and allow us to extend our results to the district and school stakeholders. This distinction is important because throughout the legislation, program efficacy is generally what is required; however, conducting an RCT in real schools on a limited budget, and with real teachers who have varying levels of implementation, represents an effectiveness trial more than an efficacy trial.

Meeting SBR Requirements During Program Development. Publishing houses generally focus their scientific research efforts annually on the K–12 programs covering reading, mathematics, and science. The number of programs released each year is dictated by the adoption cycle, but the average large publishing house typically publishes two or three new programs per year. This means that six or seven other programs may be in development in the same year and undergoing development research but not ready for release. With the advent of NCLB, publishers not only have to simultaneously develop multiple products, but now must steep each product in SBR (some of which is addressed within publishing houses, while some is built on existing high-quality research).

Scientific research issues related to program development can be complex thanks to the competitiveness among the large publishing houses and the need to protect their intellectual property and investments. From conversation with colleagues in other publishing houses and responses made to the National Math Panel regarding research that supports math programs (National Math Panel transcript, 2006), the description given here offers readers a realistic account of research likely to happen. This should not be construed as a definitive method that occurs for every program with every publisher.

Program development generally proceeds in five primary stages. First, a comprehensive literature review, initiated by both the authorship and the editorial teams, is conducted to analyze current research. The purpose of this literature review is to establish best instructional practices in the appropriate content area for integration into the new program, establish a basis in rigorous research, and review the copyright(s) of the program so previous strategies that have proven effective can be carried over into the new program.

Second, the editors concurrently begin identifying state and national standards. The National Math Panel recently posed the question at its September 13, 2006, meeting in Cambridge (National Math Panel transcript, 2006), "Why have textbooks seemingly grown hundreds of pages in the last ten years?" One primary reason for this growth is divergent, and increasingly specific, state standards. The publishers must work with multiple districts and states to determine their content requirements, which often leads to increased textbook size.

Third, an internal marketing research team conducts focus groups with teachers and administrators from various states and districts to identify their needs, specifically the needs of subgroups targeted by NCLB (examples are English language learners, or ELLs, and the socioeconomically disadvantaged). Questions are posed, such as, "How can we meet the diverse needs of your student population, specifically students in need of intervention and ELL support?" Potentially, a larger sample of teachers may be reached via surveys and questionnaires. An advisory board (or an expert panel) comprising researchers and practitioners advises publishers on best instructional practices, necessary resources, and appropriate content to ensure textbooks support these populations. An expert panel may also be formed to evaluate the evidence collected and make recommendations for program development.

Fourth, once a prototype (typically a small portion of the book, perhaps two or three chapters) is completed, the field-testing cycle begins. Teachers are asked to use the prototype in classrooms according to implementation guidelines established by the publisher. Continuous feedback from teachers about the quality of content, organizational structure, pacing, usability, and so forth, informs the product revision. Although this feedback provides useful formative information, very little summative research is collected during the program development cycle. In fact, summative information at this point is questionable; only a small amount of content is covered in field testing and the assessments used are typically publisher-created or subtests of a larger assessment.

NEW DIRECTIONS FOR EVALUATION • DOI: 10.1002/ev

Finally, publishers have to align their textbooks to state standards, especially because each state must have documentation that demonstrates the content alignment (that is, both depth and breadth) between the textbook and their state standards. This verifies to states that textbooks contain the necessary materials to cover all content that is tested on their state exams. Additionally, some publishers have also begun to align their curriculum- embedded assessments to state standards. This method is still fairly new, but some states do require this alignment.

In summary, it is difficult to describe the role of research in program development prior to NCLB because it varied widely across publishers and programs. There was ongoing research conducted to support development of programs, but it was typically not as rigorous as experimental studies. Except for programs funded by the National Science Foundation (Everyday Mathematics; Investigations in Number, Data, and Space), the majority of publisher-supported research after NCLB has largely focused on formative data collected from field tests using such methods as focus groups, surveys, questionnaires, and some quasi-experimental studies. However, the trend is to moving toward conducting more experimental studies within the product development stage.

Meeting SBR Requirements Postdevelopment. Once a program has been published, publishers contract with external, independent evaluators to launch an RCT on the completed product. Typically, these studies are 1 or 2 years in duration and involve randomly assigning teachers to use either the new textbook or what is existing at the school site. Although most researchers working with publishers on efficacy studies generally follow the research guidelines developed by the WWC, formative data is also collected from participating teachers and is used to inform development of new programs. The cycle of research is continuous, designed not only to document program effectiveness, but also to provide constructive feedback regarding product usage from teachers and administrators. The process describing how RCTs can be conducted in educational settings has been discussed elsewhere (Mosteller & Boruch, 2002); therefore, a detailed description of the stages for conducting an RCT is not found in this chapter. In the next section, however, we discuss the challenges of implementing these studies in school settings.

Complexities That Occur as a Result of Driving Influences

The driving influences of the WWC (via SBR requirements) and textbook adoptions pose significant challenges to publishers, notably, timing adoption cycles appropriately across 50 states, the reality of conducting experimental research in schools, and having these disparate programs of research adequately address the needs of multiple stakeholders.

NEW DIRECTIONS FOR EVALUATION • DOI: 10.1002/ev

Adoption Cycles. Although some argue that RCTs constitute the most rigorous test of program impact (Boruch, de Moya, & Snyder, 2002), numerous complications arise from implementing quality RCTs across curriculum programs. First, quality scientific research takes time, which is often not available, given the adoption cycles and the product development that must occur prior to release of a new product. Second, any new educational program is at a disadvantage to demonstrate student achievement gains during the first year of publication, primarily because teachers (implementing the program for the first time) are compared to a group of teachers who have implemented an existing curriculum for as much as the last several years. Third, it is difficult to respond to requests for proposals (RFPs) from states that require RCTs while in the first year of publication. Typically, publishers can only offer a statement of work from the independent researcher to demonstrate that an efficacy study is under way. In many states, this is not considered adequate and the publisher is excluded from the adoption list for that year. Fourth, many states have a policy that allows adoption only of textbooks that have been copyrighted within 3 to 5 years of the adoption year. Finally, all states receive a national version of the textbook, except California, Texas, and Florida; each of these states requires customized reading, mathematics, and science programs to meet its unique state standards. This complicates the adoption cycles tremendously, especially for these three large states.

The Reality of Conducting Research in Schools. The WWC has begun citing program effectiveness evidence from studies that use strong quasi-experimental designs, but the pressure remains to conduct RCTs in schools. However, the complication of conducting RCTs at schools raises issues for researchers and publishers. First, there is no true control group when working on core programs. The researchers must acknowledge that a control group includes those students and teachers using an existing textbook. Second, although randomization in schools should take place at the student level, this requirement is nearly impossible in studying a core reading, mathematics, or science program. Even if this were feasible, schools typically have a rationale or criteria for assigning some students to certain teachers or classes. Nevertheless, it is possible for evaluators to conduct student-level random assignment in evaluating intervention programs.

There are advantages to participating in a research study (free educational materials, professional development, monetary stipends for teachers, and so on), but schools struggle with having half of their teachers randomly assigned to using a new product because this prevents all the teachers at the school from collaborating throughout the year. Even though it is done to avoid contamination, it is critical that control teachers not plan together with treatment teachers. Schools also struggle with having two or more products being used at the same school within the same grade level, which may raise equity issues for students and their parents. The additional class time spent administering assessments related to the study imposes on schools the challenge of covering required content in fewer days.

Teachers struggle with a different set of challenges. Treatment teachers are asked to follow best-practice implementation guidelines that were developed by the author, editorial, and research teams. This can create more planning time than normal during their year in the study. In addition, treatment teachers may spend more time than control teachers completing checklists that document their program usage throughout the year. Also, treatment teachers must participate in professional development training on the new program while their colleagues can continue using their existing program.

Alternatively, there are also ethical challenges associated with denying some teachers and groups of students exposure to a new program. Control teachers may be using a textbook that is old (to relate an example, one of our control teachers had a book with a story about the possibility of going to the moon). If the district allows teachers to help choose textbooks for their school, the control teachers will not have the benefit of using the materials for a year to help make their decision. The control teachers also miss out on additional professional development that is offered to the treatment teachers. Publishers tend to offer the test materials to the control group teachers at the end of the school year, but the offer of professional development varies with the study. Together, these conditions can generally lead to frustration from teachers participating in research studies.

Responding to a Diverse Group of Stakeholders. As we acquire more experience conducting scientific research in public school districts, we gain further insight into the consequences of our work. One large consequence of increasing programs of research in publishing houses is the need to address a variety of stakeholders with a limited number of research studies. The publisher's stakeholders include the federal government, state departments of education, districts, schools, administrators, teachers, parents, and—most important—students. It is a continuing challenge for all publishers to determine how to meet the needs of these stakeholders across the program of research.

Complex interaction of variables must be considered by publishers. For example, NCLB has emphasized the necessity of SBR, which resulted in a call for an organization that performs the functions of the WWC. NCLB also created new guidelines that affected textbook adoption. As a result, there was an increased demand for rigorous, systematic research to support product development and demonstrate product efficacy. Given the changing nature of product development and efficacy studies, the number of stakeholders and variables to study has changed. The research to support product development must address the needs of the authors, editors, marketers, designers, technology specialists, and the sales force. The research to support effectiveness must address the requirements of states, districts, administrators, teachers, students, and parents. The needs of each stakeholder may

NEW DIRECTIONS FOR EVALUATION • DOI: 10.1002/ev

vary widely but must be given appropriate consideration in the development of a rigorous research model.

Future Directions

With the requirements imposed on publishers by NCLB, many challenges, complications, and debates have been introduced into publishing houses. However, with these developments are opportunities afforded publishers. One potentially positive development in research to support program effectiveness is the extended-term mixed-method (ETMM) evaluation design proposed by Chatterji (2005). The ETMM designs follow the life span of individual programs and policy initiatives within a particular environment, employing appropriate descriptive research methods in the early states of program adoption and implementation followed by timely, judicious implementation of experimental designs at a subsequent state (Chatterji, 2005). This method would allow publishers the opportunity to determine more of the *whys* as well as the *what works*. Raudenbush (2005) argues that RCTs are the gold standard for assessing the effects of instructional intervention, but the success of the effort depends on a well-integrated, methodologically diverse research effort. It is hoped that these arguments will continue to be heard in the education research community so that we can further embrace a mixed-methods approach in the publishing community while meeting government research standards.

Publishers have begun spending additional money on research, but they would need virtually unlimited resources to conduct all the research that is recommended. Given the external pressures to focus resources on external research efforts, this may lead to fewer resources available for product development. Publishers often have conversations about other questions worth exploring that are not exclusively related to program effectiveness. Good research practice dictates that the research question should guide the choice of method, not the other way around. Raudenbush (2005) stated that "experiments, while necessary, are, however, far from sufficient to support the learning required for effective instructional innovation" (p. 27). Instructional innovation must happen before program efficacy testing, and this would be most beneficial for studies that involve learning how to serve certain subpopulations, such as ELL and special education students.

Conclusion

NCLB has affected not only state departments of education, districts, and schools, but also the textbook publishers that supply these entities with educational materials. Whereas prior to NCLB research was considered a value-added endeavor, it is now ingrained into the fabric of every stage, from product development to experimental effectiveness trials in classrooms after adoption. This discourse may lead to a more granular definition of a scientific research base in program development, as seen with the guidelines established for evidence of effectiveness. It is my hope that this article sheds light on how the research process has been adapted in publishing houses given the NCLB legislation.

References

Boruch, R., de Moya, D., & Snyder, B. (2002). The importance of randomized field trials in education and related areas. In R. Boruch and F. Mosteller (Eds.), *Evidence matters: Randomized trials in education research.* Washington, DC: Brookings Institution Press.

Chatterji, M. (2005). Evidence on "What Works": An argument for extended-term mixed-method (ETMM) evaluation designs. *Educational Researcher, 34,* 14–24.

Chen, H. (2005). Practical program evaluation: Assessing and improving planning, implementation, and effectiveness. Thousand Oaks, CA: Sage.

Donaldson, S. I., Christie, C. A., & Mark, M. M. (in press). *What counts as credible evidence in applied research and contemporary evaluation practice?* Newbury Park, CA: Sage.

Mosteller, F., & Boruch, R. (2002). *Evidence matters: Randomized trials in education research.* Washington, DC: Brookings Institution Press.

National Mathematics Advisory Panel. (2006). Summary. Retrieved April 2007, from http://www.ed.gov/about/bdscomm/list/mathpanel/3rd-meeting/sum-transcript0913.pdf

No Child Left Behind Act. (2001). Public Law No. 107–110. 107th Congress, 110 *Congressional Record* 1425, 115 Stat.

Raudenbush, S. W. (2005). Learning from attempts to improve schooling: The contribution of methodological diversity. *Educational Researcher, 34,* 25–31.

Slavin, R. E. (2002). Evidence-based education policies: Transforming educational practice and research. *Educational Researcher, 31,* 15–21.

U.S. Department of Education. (2003). *Identifying and implementing educational practices supported by rigorous evidence: A user friendly guide.* Washington, DC: U.S. Department of Education, Institute of Education Sciences, National Center for Education Evaluation and Regional Assistance.

U.S. Department of Education. (2005). Scientifically based evaluation methods (RIN 1890-ZA00). *Federal Register, 70*(15), 3586–3589.

MARCY BAUGHMAN is the director of academic research at Pearson Education.

Eddy, R. M., & Berry, T. (2008). Challenges and opportunities revealed by the impact of No Child Left Behind on evaluation as a discipline. In T. Berry & R. M. Eddy (Eds.), *Consequences of No Child Left Behind for Educational Evaluation. New Directions for Evaluation, 117*, 95–103.

8

Challenges and Opportunities Revealed by the Impact of No Child Left Behind on Evaluation as a Discipline

Rebecca M. Eddy, Tiffany Berry

Abstract

The field of evaluation faces a number of serious challenges in light of No Child Left Behind legislation, among them feasibility, resources, and blurring lines among research, evaluation, and assessment. At the same time, these challenges open the door for opportunities in evaluation. Now more than ever, the expertise of evaluators is needed and the demand for well-prepared evaluators has increased. The external demands of this legislation on evaluation practice suggest multiple opportunities for research on evaluation that will extend knowledge within the discipline of evaluation. © Wiley Periodicals, Inc.

The purpose of this issue of *New Directions for Evaluation* is to address issues confronting the field of evaluation since the inception of No Child Left Behind (NCLB, 2001). In these chapters are a variety of case studies and examples that demonstrate how the legislation has influenced evaluation practice, particularly within schools, districts, and programs. We have highlighted the critical issues of consideration and debate.

NEW DIRECTIONS FOR EVALUATION, no. 117, Spring 2008 © Wiley Periodicals, Inc.
Published online in Wiley InterScience (www.interscience.wiley.com) • DOI: 10.1002/ev.255

This chapter reviews the most prominent themes found in the volume, specifically related to scientifically based research (SBR) and accountability. Although we understand that NCLB goes beyond the scope of these two pillars, they remain the aspects of the legislation that have the greatest impact on our work. These themes have been extended to include areas of challenge and opportunities for the field of evaluation.

Scientifically Based Research and Accountability

The use of SBR in NCLB is addressed in several chapters in the volume. Many of these chapters have referenced volume 113 of *New Directions for Evaluation* (Julnes & Rog, 2007) regarding the controversy over the practicality or appropriateness of using experimental methods in a variety of contexts. Beyond this debate, many of the current volume's chapter authors have reviewed the implications of this standard as it relates to their own work. In addition to SBR, changes in accountability requirements have had a tremendous impact in the field of education. Next, we present challenges related to the priority given to SBR and the changes in accountability systems under NCLB, and we analyze how these two elements interact within the current environment in evaluation. With consideration for these challenges, we then offer opportunities for the field of evaluation. These opportunities range from the practical (evaluator training) to the theoretical (the relationship between theory and practice). What follows is not an exhaustive list; we welcome additional commentary to expand our thinking and practice.

Challenges for the Discipline of Evaluation Under NCLB

NCLB presents numerous challenges to our practice. Some of the most salient themes found in the volume are identified next.

Feasibility. The first theme is one of feasibility for implementing the types of research and evaluation practice necessary in the current environment. In many of the chapters, common problems associated with programs and schools in the wake of NCLB are that some mandates are not realistic to implement in terms of time and other resources. Examples are reconciling competing accountability systems (chapter 4), prioritizing evaluation questions while satisfying multiple funding agency needs (chapter 5), using standardized test scores across multiple states with varying achievement models (chapter 6), conducting RCTs on educational products that meet strict research design specifications yet occur often enough to meet state adoption cycles (chapter 7), and the necessity of educating school and program personnel to use data effectively (chapters 3, 4, and 5). Another consideration around feasibility was raised in chapter 4, where district evaluators must simultaneously become experts in conducting SBR while meeting increased demands for accountability reporting. Our ethical responsibilities as evaluators, as outlined in the Joint Committee Standards (1994), require us to conduct evaluations that are feasible. Failing to meet these feasibility requirements ultimately wastes resources and undermines our profession.

Resources. Another theme central to this volume is acknowledgment that resource limitations (for example, time, money, and expertise) hinder an evaluator's ability to succeed under NCLB. First, some NCLB mandates assume unrealistic expectations regarding the time it takes to show improvement after programmatic changes occur. This includes time in the classroom to show improvement in test scores once teacher professional development (chapter 3) or a new curriculum (chapter 7) is implemented. It also takes time to train teachers (chapter 3) and program personnel (chapter 5) in using data to inform strategic planning. Finally, when conducting RCTs on educational products in schools (chapter 7), it takes time for teachers to implement a new curriculum with high fidelity. Within the context of an experiment, this suggests that implementation of a new curriculum may not be equivalent to what nontreatment teachers use in their classrooms. In summary, enough time must be made available to allow meaningful change to occur if we are to see positive results in student achievement.

Second, according to Mathis (2005), the federal government would need to supply an additional $6 billion to meet the requirements for administering the law. In addition to the direct costs of implementing the law, there are a variety of other monetary costs associated with completing necessary accountability tasks. For example, several chapter authors suggested that additional time and money must be available to train teachers (chapter 3), district evaluators (chapter 4), and program staff (chapter 5). Also, as seen as in chapter 3, changes observed at Torch Middle School were made possible by a large grant that provided money to the lowest performing schools through the High Priority Schools Grant Program (California Department of Education, 2007). Empirical research is required to determine whether an increase in funding has resulted in a similar level of change in other California schools. Although one can argue that increased financial resources are a necessary, though not sufficient, condition for supporting a reform environment (Iatarola & Fruchter, 2006; Springer, Houck, Ceperley, & Hange, 2007), it is clear that necessary funding must be available to allow mandated changes to become meaningful changes.

The third challenge related to resources is expertise. For example, the authors of chapter 4 suggested that district evaluators required a necessary level of expertise both to conduct and to be consumers of SBR. A similar level of expertise extends to teachers who must understand disaggregated standardized testing data as well as other forms of data that, when combined, indicate student learning patterns. Although they may be construed simultaneously as challenges and opportunities, additional expertise is required to initiate and sustain change in teacher professional practice

chapter 3), conduct experimental designs and statistical analysis (chapter 4), and access and interpret state assessment data (chapter 6).

In addition to addressing such resources, programs and schools must have other elements in place to thrive under the current system, specifically an organizational culture that supports the evaluation process (Russ-Eft & Preskill, 2001). For example, the authors in chapter 5 reported having a collaborative relationship where program and evaluation staff shared evaluation responsibilities as well as commitment to using data to inform program improvement and organizational development. The organization also supported these activities through a multiyear investment in evaluation, which allowed the evaluators to alter evaluation questions and data collection efforts over several years. Similarly, in chapter 3, the school culture facilitated shared commitment to using student assessment data to drive instruction in the classroom. Having these organizational characteristics in place may help alleviate the challenges posed by a lack of necessary resources.

Blurring the Lines Among Research, Assessment, and Evaluation. We are highly concerned that forcing an experimental design on evaluators via NCLB mandates will compromise the unique qualities in evaluation that differentiates it from both research and assessment. As several chapter authors have discussed, the shift in design preference has implications in devaluing other types of evaluation approaches and also has the potential to turn evaluation practice in education into a solely compliance-oriented endeavor (Ryan, 2005). Further, chapers 2, 3, and 6 also acknowldege that scarce resources require prioritizing learning outcomes based solely on standardized test scores. If stakeholder needs are other than compliance-oriented, yet the resources allow for only tracking accountability requirements, their competing information needs are not met.

These predetermined evaluation designs and outcomes, and a potential decrease in autonomy, hint at the greater issue of blurring the lines among research, assessment, and evaluation. Although we appreciate an increased focus on accountability and greater rigor through SBR in educational evaluation, the neglect of process and implementation monitoring is detrimental, particularly if ignoring this information prevents important feedback from reaching program managers. This feedback process has been considered a distinct activity that differentiates evaluation from research (Levin-Rozalis, 2003). Evaluators also offer particular expertise beyond conducting scientific studies, including combining multiple data sources to make definitive evaluative statements, incorporating stakeholders into the process of learning about and participating in evaluation, and tailoring evaluation questions to fit specific program needs. Further, although scientific research and evaluation share some of the same tools (for example, data collection, measurement, statistical analysis, and so forth), research lacks the fundamental qualities that have defined evaluation as a discipline, those involved in determining the merit, worth, or significance of the evaluand (Scriven, 1991).

Although SBR may be conceptually redefining evaluation as a research-driven endeavor, this reality becomes even more problematic when one examines what is happening in practice. That is, given the issues raised in this volume and including the feasibility and resource challenges expressed in this chapter, it is clear that, in some cases, educational evaluators are spending their time not on conducting SBR, but rather on such assessment duties as testing students, developing systems to store data, measuring student achievement longitudinally, and more. In fact, according to chapter 4, assessment duties are overwhelming the duties of educational evaluators given the need to comply with NCLB and their state accountability systems. If evaluation consists only of measuring student achievement scores, then evaluation becomes nothing more than an exercise in assessment or measurement, which is "(i) . . . characteristically not concerned with merit, only with 'purely descriptive' properties, and (ii) those properties are characteristically unidimensional, which avoids the need for the integrating step" (Scriven, 1991, p. 139). Although assessment is an important component of an evaluator's work, we are increasingly concerned that the lines are blurring among evaluation, research, and assessment, given SBR mandates and the practical reality of complying with current student testing accountability requirements.

Opportunities for the Discipline of Evaluation Revealed in NCLB

Although the challenges related to SBR and accountability demands found in this volume may be difficult to navigate, NCLB also affords multiple opportunities to the discipline of evaluation. With the assumption that the NCLB reauthorization changes may not address our most important concerns as evaluators, we should acknowledge what the opportunities of our discipline would be if the status quo remained.

Promotion of Evaluator's Expertise. The first major opportunity is that there is an increased interest in our work to think about and use data, specifically the current emphasis in education programs (chapter 5), schools (chapter 3), and publishers (chapter 7). In this third example, textbook publishers are now conducting research studies on published curriculum products with more regularity than they have in previous years. This research extends into product development; publishers now require skills provided by evaluators and researchers more than they did before SBR was required on educational products.

For a school- and program-based evaluation, evaluators must guide educators and program personnel through the process of data collection, analysis, and interpretation; additionally, teachers, school officials, and other program administrators must develop the requisite evaluative skills necessary to draw appropriate conclusions. Both of these situations require more training in evaluation theory and practice for a broader audience of stakeholders. For example, in chapter 3, school-site personnel had to become more proficient in using and interpreting student achievement data. However, given the complexity of tracking data across multiple years or interpreting student achievement for multiple cohorts (chapter 6), this process could be facilitated by a professional evaluator who possesses the technical skills to guide stakeholders through the maze of requirements and moving accountability targets.

A final area of expertise is related to the opportunity to promote evaluator skills around data management. Several chapters addressed data management needs as central to their concerns in successfully navigating a post-NCLB environment. For example, the authors of chapter 4 described how not having an efficient data-management system can be a hindrance to schools and districts. In chapter 3, an organized data-management system was a central component of progress achieved at the middle school. The authors of chapter 5 described how their community-based organization was able to collaborate with the school district in supplying electronic data to track students in programs. These descriptions suggest that evaluators, school districts, schools, and programs must have efficient processes in place, particularly access to electronic data and ways to organize these data effectively. Evaluators typically have particular expertise in facilitating the organization, analysis, and reporting of data that schools, districts, and programs are required to collect.

Evaluator Training. To be competitive in publishing houses or to garner additional federal, state, or private funding, evaluation is becoming a necessary condition for success. The chapter authors have given examples where schools, districts, and organizations redistributed resources toward internal and external evaluation activities. In response to the increased call for skilled evaluators comes the importance of training evaluators. There has been debate surrounding evaluation training and appropriate evaluator competencies for years (Altschuld, 1999; Stevahn, King, Ghere, & Minnema, 2005). It is largely, though not uniformly, agreed that evaluators should possess a core set of competencies and skills required for "entry into the club" (Scriven, 1996). A specific attempt to establish evaluator competencies involved creating a checklist of essential competencies for program evaluators (Stevahn et al., 2005), which details core competencies, such as professional practice, systematic inquiry, interpersonal competence, and so forth. However, given the complexity that is apparent in any discussion of NCLB and evaluation, educational evaluators may need to go beyond these general skills to perform their jobs effectively. For example, chapter 4 illustrates the necessity for all those working within the school system to have sufficient skill in understanding and navigating competing accountability systems. In addition, evaluators working with any longitudinal or student achievement data must appreciate the critical issues with assessment outlined in chapter 6 and respond with appropriate analyses and interpretations. Also, an evaluator's ability to effectively educate and train clients

New Directions for Evaluation • DOI: 10.1002/ev

in accountability systems as well as the discipline of evaluation (chapters 3 and 5) is not a trivial matter. All of these issues must be considered in appropriately identifying evaluator competencies for those working within the current system.

Research on Evaluation. Finally, this volume opens fertile ground for research on evaluation. In response to accountability frameworks and increased emphasis on evidenced-based practice, much more empirical work should be done on how evaluation practitioners (1) conceptualize evaluation, (2) practice it, (3) operationalize the relationship between evaluation theory and practice, and (4) understand how evaluator background variables (for example, content expertise, training, and the like) interact with the context in which evaluators work. This section explores these issues so that the evaluation field can begin to document the multidirectional relationships among evaluator experience, the evaluation context in which they operate, and evaluation as a discipline.

First, it is important to examine how practicing evaluators conceptualize evaluation under NCLB. For example, the current accountability mandates require mapping student performance to content standards, determining appropriate performance bands (that is, advanced, proficient, basic, and so on), and measuring student progress. Each is conceptually similar to three of the four key components within Scriven's perspective (1986) on the logic of valuing, although this process misses the fourth essential component of synthesizing these results into a value statement about the evaluand. Given this, it is important to examine whether evaluators have begun to incorporate the process of valuing into their activities. Have these thoughts trickled over to evaluation practice? Do evaluators value measuring student performance against an existing standard? Do they find this approach limiting and, in fact, counter to measuring real student progress? The answer to this question depends on the extent to which that standard or value is sound, reasonable, justified, and appropriate. Although the methods that evaluators use in practice are often constrained by the current experimental zeitgeist in educational research (Julnes & Rog, 2007), this could be a fruitful area of research for those interested in evaluators' conceptual framework of evaluation.

Second, the chapters offer several illuminating examples of how evaluation practice has been adapted under NCLB, as with greater focus on student achievement data (chapter 5), building evaluation capacity within schools (chapter 3), increased use of sophisticated statistical analyses such as hierarchical linear modeling (chapter 4), and tracking individual student growth given state assessment data (chapter 6). Because the chapters offer rich anecdotal evidence, it is important to substantiate the extent to which these practices generalize not only to other evaluators working within the NCLB milieu, but also to evaluators working in other evidenced-based disciplines.

Third, given the recent work conducted by Christie (2003) examining the relationship between theory and practice, the field would benefit from studying longitudinally how practitioners' theoretical approaches change over time. For example, it is possible that evaluation theories have become less relevant to educational evaluators than even the existing evaluation literature would indicate (Christie, 2003). Alternatively, the quantitative methodological approach espoused in SBR may begin to gain ground while pushing out other competing evaluation theories (that is, participatory, use-oriented, and others). Or perhaps evaluators have begun to define their role as an assessment specialist specifically, rather than more globally as an evaluator. These issues are worthy of empirical study, especially if, as Chen (2005) indicates, evaluation practitioners need more support in using contingency theories of evaluation rather than consistently applying one universal theory to guide evaluation practice.

Finally, given the opportunities for the discipline of evaluation that we have described (specifically, evaluator training and expertise), it is time we think critically about the most appropriate training models and evaluator expertise for the context in which evaluators work. Are global skills related to the core competencies for evaluators enough for evaluators to perform their duties successfully under heavier accountability requirements? Are specialized skills, specific to certain disciplines, necessary for evaluators to thrive? Analyzing how evaluator background variables interact with the context in which they operate is another area of fruitful research.

Conclusion

In conclusion, we believe this volume lays fertile ground for continued discussion about the consequences of accountability frameworks for the evaluators and clients they serve. Many of the challenges, impacts, and consequences identified throughout the volume are reasonable claims from practitioners working in the field of educational evaluation. There is ample opportunity for evaluators to study how the discipline of evaluation has been influenced by implementation of NCLB as well as other systems that promote evidenced-based practice. With changes that have occurred in conjunction with, and as a consequence of, NCLB, we can ponder what our practice would look like tomorrow if we were suddenly free from the stringent AYP requirements dictated by NCLB or had much wider definitions of SBR as it relates to funding priorities. As a field, would we change our practice substantially? Would students learn more or less? Would educators feel less accountable for students' performance? Would teachers, students, and parents have a higher level of satisfaction with their school? Would local programs have fundamentally different evaluation questions than they do now? As our field and our understanding continue to grow, we hope that our humble effort will facilitate ongoing conversation regarding the theoretical and practical responsibilities we have as evaluators.

References

Altschuld, J. (1999). The certification of evaluators: Highlights from a report submitted to the board of directors of the American Evaluation Association. *American Journal of Evaluation, 20,* 481–493.

California Department of Education. (2007). *HPSGP, II/USP, and CSR resources.* Retrieved July 19, 2007, from http://www.cde.ca.gov/ta/lp/hp/resources.asp

Chen, H. (2005). Practical program evaluation: Assessing and improving planning, implementation, and effectiveness. Thousand Oaks, CA: Sage.

Christie, C. A. (2003). *The practice-theory relationship in evaluation. New Directions for Evaluation, 97.*

Iatarola, P., & Fruchter, N. (2006). An alternative method for measuring cost-effectiveness: A case study of New York City's Annenberg challenge. *Journal of Education Finance, 31,* 276–296.

Joint Committee on Standards for Educational Evaluation. (1994). *The program evaluation standards.* Thousand Oaks, CA: Sage.

Julnes, G., & Rog, D. J. (2007). *Informing federal policies on evaluation methodology: Building the evidence base for method choice in government sponsored evaluation. New Directions for Evaluation, 113.*

Levin-Rozalis, M. (2003). Evaluation and research: Differences and similarities. *Canadian Journal of Program Evaluation, 18,* 1–31.

Mathis, W. J. (2005). The cost of implementing the federal No Child Left Behind Act: Different assumptions, different answers. *Peabody Journal of Education, 80,* 90–119.

No Child Left Behind Act. (2001). Public Law No. 107–110. 107th Congress, 110 *Congressional Record* 1425, 115 Stat.

Russ-Eft, D., & Preskill, H. (2001). *Evaluation in organizations: A systematic approach to enhancing learning, performance, and change.* New York: Basic Books.

Ryan, K. (2005). Making educational accountability more democratic. *American Journal of Evaluation, 26,* 532–543.

Scriven, M. (1986). New frontiers of evaluation. *Evaluation Practice, 7,* 7–44.

Scriven, M. (1991). *Evaluation thesaurus* (4th ed.). Thousand Oaks, CA: Sage.

Scriven, M. (1996). Types of evaluation and types of evaluator. *Evaluation Practice, 17,* 151–161.

Springer, M. G., Houck, E. A., Ceperley, P. E., & Hange, J. (2007). Revenue generation and resource allocation and deployment practices in smaller learning communities: Lessons learned from three high schools. *Journal of Education Finance, 32,* 443–469.

Stevahn, L., King, J. A., Ghere, G., & Minnema, J. (2005). Establishing essential competencies for program evaluators. *American Journal of Evaluation, 26,* 43–59.

REBECCA M. EDDY *is an evaluator of educational programs and research assistant professor in the School of Behavioral and Organizational Sciences at Claremont Graduate University.*

TIFFANY BERRY *is a practicing educational evaluator and research assistant professor in the School of Behavioral and Organizational Sciences at Claremont Graduate University.*

NEW DIRECTIONS FOR EVALUATION • DOI: 10.1002/ev

INDEX

NEW DIRECTIONS FOR EVALUATION
Order Form
SUBSCRIPTIONS AND SINGLE ISSUES

DISCOUNTED BACK ISSUES:

Use this form to receive **20% off** all back issues of New Directions for Evaluation. All single issues priced at **$21.60** (normally $29.00)

TITLE   ISSUE NO.   ISBN

_____   _____   _____

_____   _____   _____

_____   _____   _____

Call 888-378-2537 or see mailing instructions below. When calling, mention the promotional code, JB7ND, to receive your discount.

SUBSCRIPTIONS: *(1 year, 4 issues)*

☐ New Order   ☐ Renewal

U.S.	☐ Individual: $85	☐ Institutional: $215
Canada/Mexico	☐ Individual: $85	☐ Institutional: $255
All Others	☐ Individual: $109	☐ Institutional: $289

Call 888-378-2537 or see mailing and pricing instructions below. Online subscriptions are available at www.interscience.wiley.com.

Copy or detach page and send to:
John Wiley & Sons, Journals Dept, 5th Floor
989 Market Street, San Francisco, CA 94103-1741

Order Form can also be faxed to: 888-481-2665

Issue/Subscription Amount: $ _____	**SHIPPING CHARGES:**
Shipping Amount: $ _____	SURFACE Domestic Canadian
(for single issues only—subscription prices include shipping)	First Item $5.00 $6.00
Total Amount: $ _____	Each Add'l Item $3.00 $1.50

(No sales tax for U.S. subscriptions. Canadian residents, add GST for subscription orders. Individual rate subscriptions must be paid by personal check or credit card. Individual rate subscriptions may not be resold as library copies.)

☐ Payment enclosed (U.S. check or money order only. All payments must be in U.S. dollars.)

☐ VISA   ☐ MC   ☐ Amex # _____ Exp. Date _____

Card Holder Name _____ Card Issue # _____

Signature_____ Day Phone _____

☐ Bill Me (U.S. institutional orders only. Purchase order required.)

Purchase order # _____

Federal Tax ID13559302   GST 89102 8052

Name_____

Address _____

Phone _____ E-mail _____

JB7ND

NEW DIRECTIONS FOR EVALUATION IS NOW AVAILABLE ONLINE AT WILEY INTERSCIENCE

What is Wiley InterScience?

Wiley InterScience is the dynamic online content service from John Wiley & Sons delivering the full text of over 300 leading scientific, technical, medical, and professional journals, plus major reference works, the acclaimed Current Protocols laboratory manuals, and even the full text of select Wiley print books online.

What are some special features of Wiley InterScience?

Wiley Interscience Alerts is a service that delivers table of contents via e-mail for any journal available on Wiley InterScience as soon as a new issue is published online.
Early View is Wiley's exclusive service presenting individual articles online as soon as they are ready, even before the release of the compiled print issue. These articles are complete, peer-reviewed, and citable.
CrossRef is the innovative multi-publisher reference linking system enabling readers to move seamlessly from a reference in a journal article to the cited publication, typically located on a different server and published by a different publisher.

How can I access Wiley InterScience?

Visit http://www.interscience.wiley.com.

Guest Users can browse Wiley InterScience for unrestricted access to journal Tables of Contents and Article Abstracts, or use the powerful search engine.
Registered Users are provided with a *Personal Home Page* to store and manage customized alerts, searches, and links to favorite journals and articles. Additionally, Registered Users can view free Online Sample Issues and preview selected material from major reference works.
Licensed Customers are entitled to access full-text journal articles in PDF, with select journals also offering full-text HTML.

How do I become an Authorized User?

Authorized Users are individuals authorized by a paying Customer to have access to the journals in Wiley InterScience. For example, a University that subscribes to Wiley journals is considered to be the Customer.
Faculty, staff and students authorized by the University to have access to those journals in Wiley InterScience are Authorized Users. Users should contact their Library for information on which Wiley journals they have access to in Wiley InterScience.

ASK YOUR INSTITUTION ABOUT WILEY INTERSCIENCE TODAY!

Research Methods and Evaluation Books of Interest

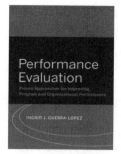

Performance Evaluation
Proven Approaches for Improving Program and Organizational Performance

Ingrid J. Guerra-Lopez
Paperback, 250 pages
ISBN 978-0-7879-8883-8

Using this resource, readers will be able to implement the most appropriate scientifically based evaluations model in a variety of situations. It offers a guide for practitioners, researchers, and educators for the understanding and application of scientifically based evaluations that are both rigorous and flexible. The book covers seven major evaluation models and the author, a highly experienced academic and consultant evaluator, bridges the gap between theory and practice by illustrating the various approaches in simple language. The book explores the research evidence behind the utility of each model, shows how each approach looks in practice, and explains why it works for one situation and not another. Academically, the author is rooted in both education and public administration, areas that often share evaluation and needs assessment courses.

Ingrid J Guerra-Lopez is an associate research professor at the Sonora Institute of Technology in Mexico and consults for public and private organizations, specifically in the areas of performance measurement and tracking.

Evaluator Competencies
Standards for the Practice of Evaluation in Organizations

Darlene F. Russ-Eft, Marcie J. Bober, Ileana de la Teja,
Marguerite Foxon, Tiffany A. Koszalka
Hardcover, 200 pages
ISBN 978-0-7879-9599-7

This guide to evaluator competencies will enhance the effectiveness of evaluators in training and in practice. Written by a team of experts in the area of evaluation and sponsored by the leading organization for performance standards (International Board of Standards for Training, Performance, and Instruction), *Evaluator Competencies* presents validated evaluator competencies with practical and applicable description of each of these competencies. The book discusses the challenges and obstacles in conducting such evaluations within dynamic, changing organizations, and provides methods and strategies for putting these competencies to use. The book also identifies alternative approaches to overcoming these challenges and obstacles.

Darlene Russ-Eft, Ph.D., is Associate Professor within the Department of Adult Education and Higher Education Leadership within the College of Education at Oregon State University. Her teaching focuses on program evaluation, research methods, and learning theory.

Program Evaluation in Practice
Core Concepts and Examples for Discussion and Analysis

Dean T. Spaulding
Paperback, 368 pages
ISBN 978-0-7879-8685-8

This ground-breaking book of teaching cases covers the essentials of program evaluation. A wide variety of evaluation projects are discussed, analyzed, and reflected upon. The book covers the essentials of program evaluation, including foundation and types of evaluation, tools for collecting data, writing reports, and sharing findings. Individual cases cover classroom instruction, community-based program, teacher training, professional development, a secondary-school based program, after-school program, reading achievement, school-improvement grant, and confidentiality.

Each case includes learning objectives, program description, evaluation plan, summary of evaluation activities and findings, key concepts, discussion questions, class activities, and suggested reading. As useful for students as it is for evaluators in training, it is a must-have for those aspiring to become effective evaluators.

Dean T. Spaulding teaches at the College of Saint Rose in Albany, New York. He is the chair of the Teaching Evaluation SIG for the American Evaluation Association.

Youth Participatory Evaluation
Strategies for Engaging Young People

Kim Sabo Flores
Paperback, 208 pages
ISBN 978-0-7879-8392-5

This groundbreaking book explores why youth participatory evaluation (YPE) has become so important so quickly. A "how to" guide to participatory research and evaluation, it provides step-by-step, playful, and accessible activities that have proven effective and can be used by evaluators, educators, youth workers, researchers, funders, and children's and human rights advocates in their efforts to more effectively engage young people.

Positioning program evaluation as a fundamental piece of the participatory research field, it includes everything from history to theory to core concepts to practical tips—a complete approach to effective participatory research and evaluation with youth. It also offers substantial theory and experience to provide a fundamental component of professional preparation and leading-edge practice.

Kim Sabo is the founder of Kim Sabo Consulting, a research and evaluation organization that focuses on participatory planning and evaluation for nonprofit organizations. She previously served on the faculty of the Graduate School of the City University of New York.

Research Methods and Evaluation Books of Interest

Mixed Methods in Social Inquiry

Jennifer C. Greene
Paperback, 232 pages
ISBN: 978-0-7879-8382-6

"An excellent addition to the literature of integrated methodology . . . The author has skillfully integrated diverse ways of thinking about mixed methods into a comprehensive and meaningful framework. She makes it easy for both the students and the practitioners to understand the intricate details and complexities of doing mixed methods research."
—ABBAS TASHAKKORI, Frost Professor and coordinator, educational research and evaluation methodology, Department of Educational and Psychological Studies, Florida International University, founding coeditor, *Journal of Mixed Methods Research*

"This is the best available book on the topic for both scholars and students."
—MARY LEE SMITH, regents professor, Arizona State University

Jennifer Greene is professor in quantitative and evaluative research methodologies, Department of Educational Psychology, College of Education, at the University of Illinois, Champaign.

Designing and Constructing Instruments for Social Research and Evaluation

David Colton, Robert W. Covert
Paperback, 412 pages
ISBN: 978-0-7879-8784-8

A comprehensive step-by-step guide to creating effective surveys, polls, questionnaires, customer satisfaction forms, ratings, checklists, and other instruments. This book can be used by those who are developing instruments for the first time and those who want to hone their skills.

This book provides a thorough presentation of instrument construction, from conception to development and pretesting of items, formatting the instrument, administration, and, finally, data management and presentation of the findings. Included are guidelines for reviewing and revising the questionnaire to enhance validity and reliability, and for working effectively with stakeholders such as instrument designers, decision-makers, agency personnel, clients, and raters or respondents.

David Colton, Ph.D., is adjunct professor and Robert W. Covert, Ph.D., is associate professor at the University of Virginia's Curry School of Graduate Studies in the program in Research, Statistics, and Evaluation.

Research Methods and Evaluation Books of Interest

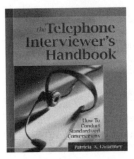

The Telephone Interviewer's Handbook
How to Conduct Standardized Conversations

Patricia A. Gwartney
Paperback, 336 pages
ISBN 978-0-7879-8638-4

This essential resource offers training on all aspects of conducting telephone interviews. It reviews the types of surveys, the interviewer's role in the survey process, survey research, ethics, laws that protect telephone interviewing, and respondents' rights. It also details the job of interviewing, including respondent selection procedures and addressing respondents' concerns about a wide range of situations. The book highlights how to record dial attempts, how to input respondents' answers, how to move from screen to screen, and how to read and evaluate call histories. It offers universal guidelines, such as common problems implementing the call disposition codes recommended by major professional associations. The author discusses interviewers' responsibilities, explaining their key role in the survey process, and how to motivate them to do their best. A special section addresses the persons who hire, train, monitor, coordinate, and supervise telephone interviewers.

Patricia A. Gwartney, Ph.D., is Professor of Sociology at the University of Oregon, Eugene. An internationally known expert in the field of survey research, she was the Founding Director of the University of Oregon Survey Research Laboratory (OSRL).

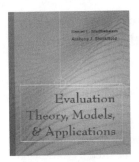

Evaluation Theory, Models & Applications

Daniel L. Stufflebeam, Anthony J. Shinkfield
Hardcover, 768 pages
ISBN: 978-0-7879-7765-8

This comprehensive resource helps you develop a commanding knowledge of the evaluation field: its history, theory, standards, models, approaches, and procedures. You'll learn to identify, analyze, and judge 26 evaluation approaches and apply standards to discriminate among legitimate and illicit approaches.

A textbook and a handbook, it includes down-to-earth procedures, checklists, and illustrations of how to carry out a sequence of essential evaluation tasks; identify and assess evaluation opportunities; prepare an institution to support a projected evaluation; design, budget, and contract evaluations; collect, analyze, and synthesize information; and report and facilitate use of findings.

Daniel L. Stufflebeam, Ph.D., is Distinguished University Professor and Harold and Beulah McKee Professor of Education at Western Michigan University, Kalamazoo.

Anthony J. Shinkfield, Ed.D., has served in numerous positions in education leadership, including assistant director, Research and Planning Directorate, Education Department of South Australia.